HOW TO MAKE
JEWELLERY
CHARMS
FROM
POLYMER
CLAY

HOW TO MAKE
JEWELLERY
CHARMS
FROM
POLYMER
CLAY

Jessica Sharpe

APPLE

A QUARTO BOOK

First published in the UK in 2014 by
Apple Press
74–77 White Lion Street
London N1 9PF

www.apple-press.com

ISBN: 978-1-84543-544-8

Conceived, designed and produced by
Quarto Publishing plc
The Old Brewery
6 Blundell Street
London N7 9BH

QUA: MPCC

Editor: Claire Waite Brown
Senior Art Editor: Emma Clayton
Designer: Jo Bettles
Photographer: Phil Wilkins
Picture Researcher: Sarah Bell
Proofreader: Sarah Hoggett
Indexer: Helen Snaith
Art Director: Caroline Guest
Creative Director: Moira Clinch
Publisher: Paul Carslake

Colour separation in Hong Kong by
Bright Arts (HK) Ltd
Printed by 1010 Printing
International Ltd, China

Contents

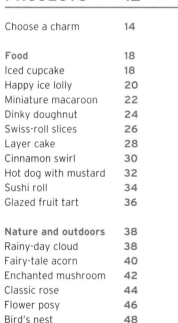

About this book

This book features 50 different projects, most of them with one or two variations. The charms range from little botanicals to special-occasion charms. What the projects have in common is that they are cute, colourful and, often, easy to make. No project uses much clay, so you can make use of your scraps.

CHOOSE A CHARM
Pages 14-17

Over four pages, the charms are shown next to each other in the order they appear in the book. Just find one you like and turn to the relevant page.

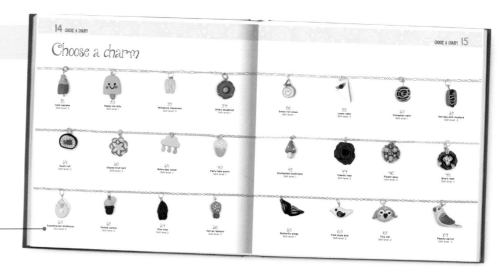

Skill level
Find a charm you like and a skill level you are comfortable with.

MATERIALS, TOOLS AND TECHNIQUES
Pages 118-141

This chapter describes types of polymer clay, the basic toolkit for working clay and tools that are used repeatedly when making charms. The techniques part of this chapter summarizes the core techniques that you will use again and again when making polymer clay charms. Use this chapter as a refresher course if you need to brush up your skills or if you are a beginner who needs to understand some of the basic polymer clay techniques.

PROJECTS Pages 12-117

The 50 projects are organized into themed groups, such as food, animals and special occasions. There is a good selection within each group, so you've got lots of choices.

Tools and materials
Each project includes a list of the colours and the tools used.

Size guide
Each project includes an actual-size photograph of a finished charm with the charm's dimensions indicated. These dimensions are of the finished pieces, so you can use them as a guide when making the charm. You can make charms bigger than shown here, but try to keep the proportions the same.

Charms in context
Charms are shown in the context of finished charm bracelets, pendants, earring, and other jewellery items to inspire you with ideas for what kinds of accessories you might make.

62 PROJECTS ✳ ANIMALS

Tools and materials
- Mauve clay
- Purple clay
- Pastel blue clay
- Blue clay
- Turquoise clay

☑ Cocktail stick
☑ Eyepin
☑ Black permanent marker

Tiny owl

Everyone's favourite nocturnal bird is napping again! This sleepy little fellow would look wonderful on a bird-themed bracelet, perhaps with the parrot from pages 64-65, or even with other wildlife, like the little deer on pages 68-69.

1 Roll a small amount of conditioned mauve clay between your hands into an oblong shape, about 1.5 cm (⁵⁄₈ in) long and 5 mm (¹⁄₄ in) wide. Try to make the shape slightly narrower at the top than at the bottom. Use your fingers to roll two small purple teardrops, about 3 mm (¹⁄₈ in) long. Place the teardrops on either side of the body at the same height, for the wings. Gently press the wings on with a cocktail stick, then carefully lift the bottom of each one so that it flicks upward.

2 Make the eyes by rolling two balls of conditioned pastel blue clay and flattening them. Together they should be roughly the same width as the top part of the owl's body. Position them on the owl between the wings. Roll two snakes of blue clay just under 1 cm (³⁄₈ in) long. These will form the owl's feather eyebrows. Using the cocktail stick, place one end of one snake in between the eyes, then wrap it around the top of one eye and flick the other end up. Repeat for the other eyebrow.

3 Make a purple heart shape, about 3 mm (¹⁄₈ in) long, for the beak, and place it just below and between the eyes.

Use the cocktail stick to nudge the beak into position.

Skill level: ● ● ●

Actual size & dimensions

A Height 15 mm (⁵⁄₈ in)
B Width 20 mm (³⁄₄ in)
C Depth 7.5 mm (⁵⁄₁₆ in)

A

B

TINY OWL 63

Wakey wakey
To make a version that's awake, once the charm is baked simply draw on some big beautiful eyes, eyelashes and all!

4 Roll three small dots of turquoise clay, about 1 mm (¹⁄₁₆ in) round, and place them across the stomach of the owl, one in the centre and one on either side. Press the cocktail stick into the centre of each dot to secure it in place.

5 Carefully insert an eyepin into the top of the owl, using the cocktail stick to slowly guide it in. Now bake the charm, following the clay manufacturer's instructions, and leave to cool.

6 When the owl is cool, draw on his eyes. Use black permanent marker to draw a curved line, then draw small lines coming away from that line as the eyelashes.

A simple drawn-on motif finishes off the sleepy owl character.

Instead of drawing eyes, you could mould them from clay disks and circles.

Pinch ears out of the egg-shaped body.

Family tree
Now that you have the basics down, try making different owls by altering the base shape and adjusting the details.

Skill level rating system
- **1 ball:** *very few skills required. Beginners to polymer clay: start here.*
- **2 balls:** *a little bit more ability is required than for one ball.*
- **3 balls:** *these projects are a little more intricate. Try these once you have had a bit of practice.*

Step-by-step photographs
The how-to process shows the charms enlarged, so you can see in detail how to make them.

Variations
Lots of the charms have ideas for variations, perhaps something as simple as altering the colour of the clay, but sometimes using a different technique or changing the design of the charm in some way.

Jessica's World

From a very young age I have used polymer clay to express myself creatively, and as I got older I incorporated the clay into my schoolwork and now my university degree. The more I work with the clay, the more I understand what it is capable of. Polymer clay is a wonderful medium that is easy to work with: with very little specialist equipment required, it truly is a craft for anyone. It can be used to create anything you could want, from jewellery, to bags, to vases and figurines. The possibilities are endless, and that's why working with it will always be a favourite craft of mine.

The more you play and work with polymer clay, the more you learn, and your skills are always improving, which is the most rewarding part.

I work at home in the studio I share with my mum, where she runs courses through her business, The Make it Room. This is also where I teach

The entrance
to the studio

polymer clay workshops throughout the year. Our studio is located outside our house and is a dream place to work in, with lots of space and natural light. Another benefit of working at home is that my dog Bramley is there too, for whenever I feel a little down!

My inspirations come from my surroundings, both in the craft world at home and my fashion university course in London. These two areas push me to create new and innovative pieces as well as more traditional charms.

I also make and sell my jewellery online and keep all information on my blog Time for Tea Beads, so to keep up-to-date with what I am doing, check in with my Etsy store to see what's new! The charms I make usually use bright, bold colours and clean shapes and lines.

Polymer clay is used worldwide and is gaining in popularity every day. There are many other artists worldwide who create poly clay charms using this versatile medium, and over the page are a few examples of what can be achieved with some practice.

Some of my charms

Bramley the dog

Sherri Kellberg *likes to mix her own colour blends, which makes her jewellery unique. For these bracelets, she created her own moulds using various objects impressed into raw polymer clay blocks.*

Nadia Michaux *used a needle to add texture on these doughnut earrings. Her general advice is to pre-bake the delicate parts before putting them together into a single piece, since polymer clay can be baked several times.*

Sue Heaser's *favourite tool for small-scale projects is a large, blunt wool needle. The matryoshka dolls were sculpted in wood-coloured clay. Brown, ochre, orange, white and black clays were used for the owls.*

Nathalie Tanghe *hasn't used a particular technique here, apart from good kneading to make the clay pliable. Her tip to subtle colours is to make good use of white clay for mixing.*

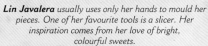

Lin Javalera usually uses only her hands to mould her pieces. One of her favourite tools is a slicer. Her inspiration comes from her love of bright, colourful sweets.

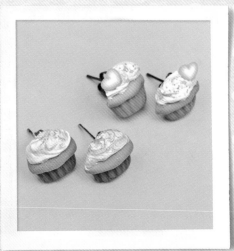

Pertrina Marie Pigrum to make the icing, Petrina mixed polymer clay with translucent liquid clay. When the clay was the right consistency, the icing was applied in a swirl pattern.

Paulina Negrete Marin's secret is perseverance, and she advises cleaning any dirt or dark spots on the clay with a small brush and acetone, which will not fade or wash the colour out.

Kat Davies likes to mix colours herself to make her subjects look more realistic and to achieve the desired shade. For the cakes here, Kat used a sewing needle and picked at the clay to create the texture.

1 Projects

The following chapter features 50 charms for you to make, organized into themed categories from food to special occasions. Step-by-step instructions for how to make each charm are accompanied by variation ideas and finished bracelets, necklaces, brooches or rings. The charms are also displayed together over the next four pages, to help you make your selection.

Choose a charm

18
Iced cupcake
Skill level: 2

20
Happy ice lolly
Skill level: 1

22
Miniature macaroon
Skill level: 3

24
Dinky doughnut
Skill level: 1

34
Sushi roll
Skill level: 2

36
Glazed fruit tart
Skill level: 3

38
Rainy-day cloud
Skill level: 1

40
Fairy-tale acorn
Skill level: 1

50
Scandinavian birdhouse
Skill level: 2

52
Potted cactus
Skill level: 2

54
Pine tree
Skill level 2

56
Hot-air balloon
Skill level: 3

26
Swiss-roll slices
Skill level 1

28
Layer cake
Skill level: 3

30
Cinnamon swirl
Skill level: 1

32
Hot dog with mustard
Skill level: 2

42
Enchanted mushroom
Skill level: 1

44
Classic rose
Skill level: 2

46
Flower posy
Skill level: 3

48
Bird's nest
Skill level: 3

58
Butterfly wings
Skill level: 1

60
Folk-style bird
Skill level: 2

62
Tiny owl
Skill level: 2

64
Peachy parrot
Skill level: 3

66
Pampered poodle
Skill level: 3

68
Dear dear
Skill level: 3

70
Hungry panda
Skill level: 2

72
Walking penguin
Skill level: 2

82
Cute camera
Skill level: 3

84
School pencil
Skill level: 2

86
Airmail envelope
Skill level: 2

88
Cotton reel
Skill level: 2

98
Colourwash flower
Skill level: 1

100
Textured bead
Skill level: 1

102
Circus tent
Skill level: 3

104
Celebration bunting
Skill level: 1

106
Patterned Easter egg
Skill level: 1

74
Little blue whale
Skill level: 2

76
Vintage teapot
Skill level: 3

78
Summer shoe
Skill level: 3

80
Retro alarm clock
Skill level: 3

90
Knitted heart
Skill level: 2

92
Russian doll
Skill level: 3

94
Faceted bead
Skill level: 1

96
Charming button
Skill level: 1

108
Halloween pumpkin
Skill level: 1

110
Gingerbread house
Skill level: 3

112
Christmas tree
Skill level: 1

114
Christmas stocking
Skill level: 2

116
Gift-wrapped box
Skill level: 1

Iced cupcake

Everyone's favourite tasty treat, cupcakes also make adorable charms. These delightful little cakes are a miniature must-have for your collection. Easily customizable with different colour combinations, you can create the perfect cupcake for you. And the best part is, they're fat free!

Tools & materials

- Brown clay
- Pastel pink clay
- Lilac clay

- ☑ Blade
- ☑ Eyepin

Actual size & dimensions

A Height 15 mm (⅝ in)
B Width 7.5 mm (⁵⁄₁₆ in)
C Depth 7.5 mm (⁵⁄₁₆ in)

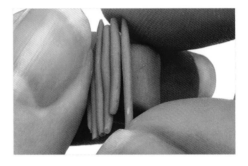

1 Roll a pea-sized ball of conditioned brown clay between your hands until smooth. Now roll 16 to 20 snakes in the same colour, about 2 mm (¹⁄₁₆ in) wide and 7.5 mm (⁵⁄₁₆ in) long.

2 Roll the ball on the work surface under one finger until it is almost cylinder shaped, and flatten the top and bottom of the shape. Place the snakes around the outside of the shape, packing them tightly next to each other so that they completely cover it.

Leave the eyepin in place to keep the charm unblocked as you add the icing.

3 Gently roll the covered cylinder under your finger to smooth the shape, then use a blade to cut the rough ends off the base.

4 Push an eyepin all the way through the centre of the shape.

Skill level: ●●●

5 Roll a snake of conditioned pastel pink clay 2 mm (¹⁄₁₆ in) wide and 10 cm (4 in) long. Place one end of the pink snake on the flat part of the cupcake base and press down gently to secure. Following the shape of the base, slowly wrap the pink clay around and up, securing as you go.

Cakes and bows
Team iced cupcakes with bows (see page 133) in coordinating colours to create a sweet little bracelet.

Move a little way further into the centre with each layer of icing.

6 Turn the cupcake base as you continue to add the icing swirl, ensuring that you leave no gaps and the overall appearance is even. Check that you are gradually moving further in towards the eyepin with each layer, so that your icing forms a nice cone shape.

Iced delights
Just like real cupcakes, charm cupcakes are brought to life by their icing. Vary the colours for the icing swirl, and experiment with different decorations.

7 Once the icing has reached the centre point, pinch off the excess clay to give a neat finish at the top. Slowly and carefully lift out the eyepin.

8 Roll small dots of lilac clay to use as sprinkles: these can be as small as 1 mm (¹⁄₃₂ in), or even smaller. Use a finger to gently press these onto the icing in random places. Bake the cupcake, following the clay manufacturer's instructions. Replace the eyepin after baking (see page 123).

Tools & materials

- Blue clay
- Tan clay
- Pastel pink clay

- ☑ Rolling pin
- ☑ 2 cm (³/₄ in) oval cutter
- ☑ Blade
- ☑ Eyepin
- ☑ Black permanent marker

Happy ice lolly

This happy little chap is perfect for the summer months - fun for any charm collector. Try making this quick-and-easy charm in a variety of colours and produce a rainbow of lolly charms.

Leave the eyepin in position to add the lolly stick in the next step.

1 Use a rolling pin to roll a smooth sheet of conditioned blue clay to an even thickness of 3 mm (¹/₈ in), about 3 cm (1¹/₄ in) long and 2 cm (³/₄ in) wide. Gently press an oval cutter through the clay and remove the cut shape.

2 Use a blade to cut a straight line about three-quarters of the way down the oval. Press slowly and steadily to ensure that the clay does not move or distort.

3 Use an eyepin to make a hole all the way through the lolly shape. Leave the eyepin in place.

Skill level:

Actual size & dimensions

A Height 15 mm (⁵⁄₈ in)
B Width 15 mm (⁵⁄₈ in)
C Depth 3 mm (¹⁄₈ in)

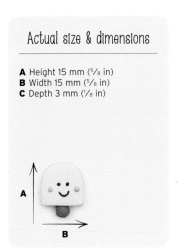

Cool characters
Coordinating cool colours emphasize the icy nature of the lolly charms. Add in a few buttons or beads to space them out.

Make sure the cheeks are level with each other.

Two dots and a smile are all that is needed to give the charm its personality.

4 Roll a small ball of tan clay, about 3 mm (¹⁄₈ in) round. Push the ball onto the eyepin at the flat end of the ice lolly and gently press the two clay shapes together. Remove the eyepin.

5 Roll two tiny pastel pink dots, about 1 mm (¹⁄₃₂ in) round, and place them on the ice lolly as the character's cheeks. Bake the charm, following the clay manufacturer's instructions.

6 Once the charm has cooled, use a black permanent marker to draw on a little smiley face for the lolly character. If you are using the lolly as a charm, replace the eyepin (see page 123), or leave out the pin and thread the charm like a bead instead.

What's in the freezer?
Like most food-based charms, lolly miniatures can be made to replicate the many different types you have in the freezer. Cut down cocktail sticks or wooden coffee stirrers to make the sticks.

Mix translucent and coloured clays for a fruity lolly.

Tools & materials

- Pastel pink clay
- Pastel pink liquid clay

- ☑ Cocktail stick
- ☑ Eyepin

Miniature macaroon

This French pâtisserie favourite is hugely popular worldwide, and using texturing techniques and liquid clay you can recreate these miniature delicacies as charms. They are intricate to make but well worth it, especially as a key piece on a Parisian-style bracelet.

Remember that the more detail you add, the more realistic the macaroon charm will appear.

1 Roll two pea-sized balls of conditioned pastel pink clay. Place each one individually between your hands and gently apply pressure to remove any cracks or uneven shaping. These will become the shells of your macaroon.

2 Press down with the pad of your finger to flatten the two balls until they are about 2 mm (¹⁄₁₆ in) thick. This will ensure that your macaroon does not look too chunky.

3 Use the point of a cocktail stick to gently press down around the base of each macaroon shell to give them their feet. Bake the shells for five minutes to make them easier to handle and less likely to be distorted in the next stages.

TIP
The shells will be hard after parbaking, so if you don't have liquid clay you can use white polymer clay as your filling instead. Make sure the clay is really soft before you apply it, and press down gently until it bulges out from the sides of the macaroon.

Skill level:

Actual size & dimensions

A Height 8 mm (⁵⁄₁₆ in)
B Width 12 mm (¹⁵⁄₃₂ in)
C Depth 12 mm (¹⁵⁄₃₂ in)

Très bien
Macaroon charms sit perfectly between pearl beads and miniature Eiffel towers on a bracelet with Parisian chic.

Don't apply too much liquid clay, since doing so will cause the two shells to slide apart.

4 Use the cocktail stick to apply a small amount of liquid clay to one of the baked shells. Aim to put on just enough so that when you press the shells together you can see the liquid clay around the edges.

5 Position an eyepin in the liquid clay: after baking, the liquid clay will hold the pin firmly in place.

6 Gently press the two macaroon halves together, taking care not to squeeze the liquid clay out of the centre. Bake fully, following the clay manufacturer's instructions.

Sophisticated French fancies
French macaroons in pastel shades are the epitome of elegance and refinement.

Tools & materials

- Brown clay
- Blue clay
- Orange clay

- ☑ Rolling pin
- ☑ 1.5 cm (⅝ in) flower cutter
- ☑ Straw
- ☑ Blade
- ☑ Eyepin

Actual size & dimensions

A Length 15 mm (⅝ in)
B Width 15 mm (⅝ in)
C Depth 7.5 mm (⁵⁄₁₆ in)

Dinky doughnut

A delicious little doughnut, with glaze and sprinkles, is a cute addition to any bracelet, and perfect for everyone: who doesn't love a doughnut after all? Making this charm is fairly simple, which means that even a complete novice can produce something worthy of being shown off.

1 Roll a ball of conditioned brown clay about the size of a marble between your hands until it is perfectly round and there are no cracks in the clay.

2 Place the ball on the work surface and press down with your finger, flattening the ball until it forms a fat disk that appears doughnut shaped.

3 Use a rolling pin to roll conditioned blue clay to the thickness of a playing card. Press a 1.5 cm (⅝ in) flower cutter into the blue clay and lift out. If the shape sticks to the work surface, use a blade to carefully lift it off.

4 Place the blue flower on top of the doughnut base. Smooth the clay to firmly fix it, working from the centre out to expel any air bubbles that will stop the clay from sticking.

Skill level: ● ● ●

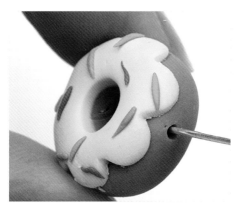

Sweet treats
A delicious doughnut makes a great accompaniment to other sweet delights, such as iced cupcakes (see pages 18–19) and bow-tie sweets (see page 133).

5 Use a straw to make the hole in the centre of the doughnut. Press the straw down slowly and evenly to make sure it goes all the way through. Then pull it straight back up, trying to maintain the doughnut's shape.

6 Roll out a thin string of conditioned orange clay, about 1 mm (1/32 in) wide. Use the blade to cut the string into sprinkles no longer than 3 mm (1/8 in).

The sprinkles should stick up a little higher than the icing.

7 Pick the sprinkles up one at a time with your finger and gently press them onto the blue clay, ensuring that they don't smudge or merge into it. Place them at different angles, as if they have been sprinkled on.

8 Gently press an eyepin through the centre of the doughnut, then remove it and bake the charm, following the clay manufacturer's instructions. Replace the eyepin after baking (see page 123).

Iced delights
Perhaps a strawberry or orange glaze is more your style, they all look good enough to eat.

Swiss-roll slices

Rolled cake charms are easy and fun to make using thin sheets of clay. This technique allows you to quickly make several charms at once, so why not make a few and share them with your friends?

Actual size & dimensions

A Height 12.5 mm (½ in)
B Width 10 mm (³/₈ in)
C Depth 7.5 mm (⁵/₁₆ in)

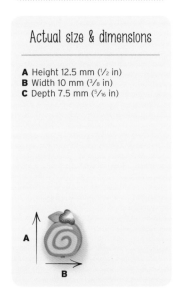

1 Roll out conditioned white and purple clay. Make each about 2 mm (¹/₁₆ in) thick and rectangular in shape, 5 x 7.5 cm (2 x 3 in). Place the white sheet on top of the purple one. Smooth from the centre of the clay out towards the edges to expel all air bubbles.

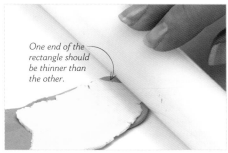

One end of the rectangle should be thinner than the other.

2 Use the rolling pin to flatten one of the narrow ends of the rectangle. A slight slope in the clay ensures a tight roll at the beginning with no air trapped inside, which would cause the clay to crack.

Start rolling from the thinner end.

3 Slowly roll the clay, making sure you roll it tightly, otherwise the swirl will not be recognizable when cut. Do not worry at this point if the clay hangs over the end of the swirl, since this will be trimmed off later.

4 When the swirl is completely rolled up, use the tips of your fingers to gently roll it back and forth across the work surface to ensure that the clay has bonded all the way through, and to force out any air.

Skill level: ● ● ●

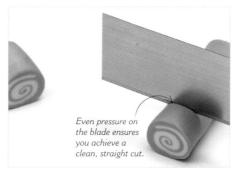

Even pressure on the blade ensures you achieve a clean, straight cut.

5 Use a blade to cut off the clay hanging over both ends of the swirl. Now measure every 7.5 mm (5/16 in) from the end to mark out the individual charms.

6 Use the blade to cut through the roll where measured. Apply even pressure to the blade to ensure the edges are as clean as possible, and press all the way through until you reach the work surface.

Tempting treats
Pair Swiss-roll and checkerboard cake slices on fishhook wires to make delicious little earrings.

Cut cubes of yellow and pink clay and wrap the checked pattern first in thin cream clay and then pastel yellow clay. Cut into slices.

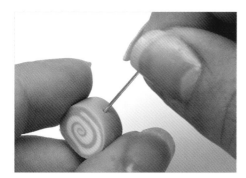

7 Use an eyepin to make a hole all the way through the charm. Slowly twist the eyepin as you gently push, to ensure that the charm does not become misshapen. Slowly and carefully remove the eyepin.

8 Now it is time to decorate! Customize your charm with a small ball of lilac clay, a green leaf shape (see page 133) and an even smaller ball of dark purple clay. Press these onto the top of the Swiss-roll slice without covering the eyepin hole. Bake the clay, following the manufacturer's instructions. Replace the eyepin after baking (see page 123).

Perfect slices
Experiment with various colours and techniques to make different sliced-cake charms for all occasions.

Layer cake

A layer cake is the ultimate celebratory treat. Used for birthdays and weddings, they look as good as they taste. Making a charm of a slice of layer cake is a little like making the real thing, since you build up a whole cake shape, then cut the slice to reveal the perfectly neat layers.

Tools & materials

- Blue clay
- White clay
- Green clay

- ☑ Rolling pin
- ☑ 2 cm (¾ in) circle cutter
- ☑ Blade
- ☑ Cocktail stick
- ☑ Eyepin

Actual size & dimensions

A Height 15 mm (⅝ in)
B Width 20 mm (¾ in)
C Depth 15 mm (⅝ in)

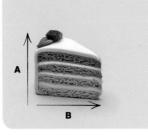

Gradually vary the shades of blue.

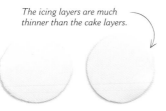

The icing layers are much thinner than the cake layers.

1 Mix four shades of blue clay by combining blue and white clay, adding more white to achieve the lighter shades. Use a rolling pin to roll each colour out to a thickness of 2 mm (¹⁄₁₆ in). Gently press a 2 cm (¾ in) round cutter individually through each shade of clay to cut out four circles.

2 Roll out a sheet of conditioned white clay to a thickness of about 1 mm (¹⁄₃₂ in), and use the cutter to cut out three circles.

Carefully smooth the icing over the cake, taking care not to dislodge the layers underneath.

3 Stack your clay circles one on top of the other, starting with the lightest blue on the bottom. Top this with a white circle, then alternate blue and white circles from light to dark, finishing with the darkest blue on the top.

4 Roll out another sheet of white clay, to a thickness of 1 mm (¹⁄₃₂ in) and about 5 cm (2 in) square. Use your fingers to gently smooth this sheet over the stack of circles, covering the top and edges. Use a blade to trim away excess clay at the base of the cake.

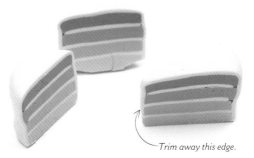

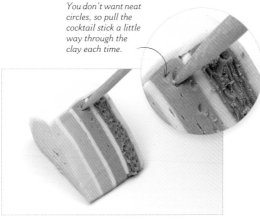

You don't want neat circles, so pull the cocktail stick a little way through the clay each time.

Use the cocktail stick to texture the biscuit base, and decorate the sides with strawberry slices (see page 137).

5 Use the blade to cut a large triangle shape out of the cake, cutting across the full width of the cake and cleanly through all layers. Neatly trim away any white clay from the point of the triangle.

Trim away this edge.

6 Rest the slice of cake on its side and press the point of a cocktail stick into the layers to add texture. Drag the cocktail stick slightly each time to create a crumb-like finish.

Cakes and biscuits
The texturing technique used to create the sponge-cake centre can also be used for biscuits and cheesecakes. Once you have tried the layer-cake charm, these are easy to achieve.

Any excuse!
Birthdays, Valentine's, parties, they all need cake. Adapt the making and decorating techniques to suit the occasion.

7 Decorate the top of the cake with a blue rose (see pages 44-45) and two green leaves (see page 133), pressing them gently onto the white clay.

8 Use the cocktail stick to insert an eyepin into the back of the cake slice. Bake the charm, following the clay manufacturer's instructions.

Use a star nozzle to extrude a swirl of 'cream'.

Add glitter to translucent clay for sparkly fillings.

Cinnamon swirl

This delightful little bun looks good enough to eat, and is the perfect charm for someone with a sweet tooth. It is quick and simple to make and uses the techniques of colouring clay with chalk pastel and glazing with varnish.

Tools & materials

- ● Beige clay
- ● Brown clay
- ● White clay

- ☑ Rolling pin
- ☑ Coarse sandpaper
- ☑ Brown chalk pastel
- ☑ Paintbrush
- ☑ Blade
- ☑ Cocktail stick
- ☑ Eyepin
- ☑ Varnish

Pour a little chalk pastel powder onto a sheet of paper and dip the paintbrush in to pick up the powder.

1 Roll a thin snake of conditioned beige clay about 7 cm (2 ³/₄ in) long and 2 mm (¹/₁₆ in) wide. Roll a snake of conditioned brown clay to the same length but slightly thinner. Don't worry if the thicknesses of the snakes vary slightly from end to end.

2 Use sandpaper to grate some brown chalk pastel into a powder and use a paintbrush to dust the powder over the beige snake so that it looks baked and golden.

3 Place the brown clay shape on top of the beige shape and gently press them together so that they stay as one.

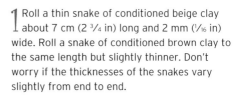

Make vanilla icing by mixing white and liquid clay to a thick consistency.

Bake some beige clay and chop it into 'nuts'.

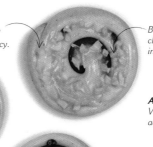

Cut a snake of brown clay into pieces to look like chocolate chips.

Added extras
Vary the basic bun by adding some tasty toppings.

Skill level: ● ● ●

A
B

Raspberry-coloured bows (see page 133) set off the bun charms.

Flavour favourites
You can also make these buns in different flavours, such as chocolate with a raspberry filling, or perhaps coffee with cream.

4 Starting at one end, coil the snakes into a spiral, making sure that the brown inner clay remains visible.

5 Continue to wind the clay until the spiral is about 1.5 cm (⁵⁄₈ in) high and wide, then use a blade to diagonally slice off the end of the shape and press this gently into the body of the swirl to fix it.

6 Roll conditioned white clay into a string, 1 mm (¹⁄₃₂ in) wide and 3 cm (1¼ in) long, and zigzag it on top of the cinnamon bun as icing. Use a cocktail stick to insert an eyepin into the top of the bun, then bake the clay, following the manufacturer's instructions. Once cooled, use the paintbrush to apply a little varnish to glaze the bun.

Lolly ring
Twist coloured clay snakes together before coiling them up in the usual way. Add a cut-off lolly stick for a realistic touch.

Use epoxy glue to fix the lolly to a flat-pad ring finding.

Hot dog with mustard

Using a few different techniques, this is a fun and relatively easy charm to make. Make it along with other favourite snack charms for a tasty themed key chain.

Actual size & dimensions

A Height 10-15 mm ($^3/_8$-$^5/_8$ in)
B Width 10 mm ($^3/_8$ in)
C Depth 5 mm ($^3/_{16}$ in)

1 For the bun, roll conditioned beige clay between your palms into a log about 1 cm ($^3/_8$ in) long and 5 mm ($^3/_{16}$ in) wide. Press gently so that the shape does not distort.

Don't cut the bun completely in half.

2 Use a blade to cut down the length of the bun, but do not cut all the way through.

Dab the brush straight down to give dots of color.

3 Use sandpaper to grate brown chalk pastel into a powder. Use a stiff brush to stipple the bun with the powder so that it is tinted and slightly dimpled, creating a baked effect.

4 Roll a thin log of conditioned burgundy clay, about 1 cm ($^3/_8$ in) long and 3 mm ($^1/_8$ in) wide. Curl up the ends of the shape by pressing it gently between your fingers.

Skill level: ●●●

Little details, like the grill lines and dimpled ends, help to make this charm so effective.

5 Place the hot-dog sausage in the bun and use black permanent marker to draw grill lines onto it. Carefully prick each end with a cocktail stick to make a small indent.

6 Roll a long, thin snake of conditioned yellow clay for the mustard, about 2 cm (³/₄ in) long and 1 mm (¹/₃₂ in) wide. Zigzag the mustard clay back and forth over the hot dog, using the cocktail stick to make minor adjustments to the positioning, since the clay is easier to control this way.

Snack time
Make a necklace inspired by junk food by placing your hot dog next to a cheeseburger.

To make a cheeseburger, start with the bun, then make the fillings and stack them all together.

7 Continue zigzagging the mustard on until the whole hot dog is covered.

8 Use the cocktail stick to insert an eyepin under the sausage and apply a little translucent liquid clay so that it stays in place. Bake the clay, following the manufacturer's instructions.

Fast-food favourites
Now that you can make hot dogs, why not try other fast foods? Simply adjust the shapes for a few of these steps to create a hamburger.

If you're not a fan of mustard, mix red and translucent clay to make ketchup instead.

Use a toothbrush to texturize the edge of the burger.

Sushi roll

With sushi gaining in popularity, this is the ideal charm for those who don't have a sweet tooth. The charm is made using a caning technique that gives the impression of individual grains of rice, plus you can make several charms at the same time.

Actual size & dimensions

A Height 13 mm (½ in)
B Width 20 mm (¾ in)
C Depth 7 mm (¼ in)

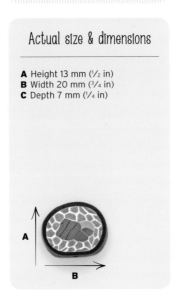

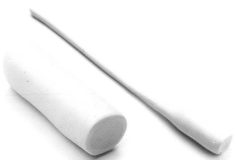

1 Roll a log of conditioned clear translucent clay, about 1 cm (³/₈ in) wide and 3 cm (1¼ in) in length. Use a rolling pin to roll a thin sheet of white clay to about 2 mm (¹/₁₆ in) thick. Wrap the log with the white sheet. Reduce the size of the wrapped log by squeezing and rolling it until it is about 1 mm (¹/₃₂ in) thick.

2 Roll a thin sheet of white clay and place on top of a cube of red clay, about 1 cm (³/₈ in) wide and deep. Use a blade to cut the stack in half and place one half on top of the other. Squeeze the stack between your fingers until the cube is about 1 cm (³/₈ in) again.

3 Partially mix some white clay with green clay (see page 128). Roll a snake from this clay, and another from dark green clay, each about 3 mm (¹/₈ in) wide and 1 cm (³/₈ in) long.

4 Stack the green snakes on top of the red cube. Use a blade to cut slices from the rice string that you made in Step 1 to the same length as the filling stack, then carefully position the rice pieces all around the filling, covering it completely.

5 Roll the sushi cane gently under your hand to smooth out all the lines and fill any gaps.

6 Roll a sheet of olive green clay to the thickness of a playing card and 10 cm (4 in) long. Wrap the sushi cane in the olive green sheet and smooth it under your hand. Trim away the excess olive green sheet.

All you can eat
Sushi rolls of various sizes on a single bracelet create a buffet feel. Coloured cords have been threaded through the chain.

7 Use a ruler and mark cutting lines on the cane, if you wish. Use the blade to cut the roll into even slices, 7 mm (¼ in) thick.

8 Use an eyepin to make a hole through the centre of the sushi slice, pressing gently so as not to distort the shape. Remove the pin and bake the charm, following the clay manufacturer's instructions. When cool, replace the eyepin (see page 123).

Smaller and smaller sushi
It is easy to create even smaller sushi rolls by reducing the whole cane (as in Step 2) before slicing.

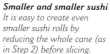

Glazed fruit tart

This delicious little tart, with realistic fruit slices and a jelly-like glaze, is charmingly delicate. Making it requires patience and practice, but persevere for stunning results. The tart base and assembly of the toppings are described here; turn to the core techniques at the back of the book for how to make the lime and strawberry fruit canes.

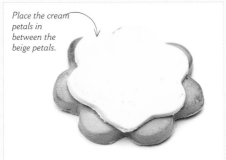

Place the cream petals in between the beige petals.

1 Use a rolling pin to roll conditioned beige clay to about 2 mm (¹⁄₁₆ in) thick, and a 1.5 cm (⅝ in) flower cutter to gently cut through the clay. Use sandpaper to grate some brown chalk pastel into a powder, then use a paintbrush to dust the powder onto the edges of the flower to achieve a baked look. Apply a light dusting of powder to the edges of the shape only.

2 Now roll out a thin layer of conditioned cream clay, about the thickness of a piece of card. Use a 1.2 cm (½ in) flower cutter to cut out the cream for the tart, and neaten the edges of the shape with your finger. Place the small cream flower on top of the larger beige flower, aiming to position the petals of the smaller flower between those of the larger one. Press gently in the centre to secure.

3 Follow the instructions on pages 136–137 to make the lime and strawberry fruit canes. Use a blade to cut thin slices of the fruit canes – four lime and six strawberry.

Skill level:

Actual size & dimensions

A Height 15 mm (⁵⁄₈ in)
B Width 15 mm (⁵⁄₈ in)
C Depth 3 mm (¹⁄₈ in)

Fruit-tart necklace
The tart on this necklace uses kiwi and grapefruit canes. Master the caning techniques on pages 136–137 and you will be able to create these fruits too.

Using a cocktail stick to position the fruit lets you see what you are doing and makes small movements easier.

The liquid clay fixes the fruit slices securely while also giving the tart a glazed finish.

4 Cut three of the lime slices in half and place these around the edge of the tart, attaching them with translucent liquid clay. Place a strawberry slice between each slice of lime. Use a cocktail stick to adjust the positioning of the fruit as necessary.

5 When the outside edge of the tart is covered with fruit slices, add the remaining whole lime slice in the centre.

6 Use the cocktail stick to help insert an eyepin into the tart base, making sure it does not distort the shape. Make sure the eyepin points downward slightly, otherwise there is a chance that it could poke through the surface of your work. Use the cocktail stick to apply translucent liquid clay on top of the fruit slices to add a lovely glaze to the finished charm, while also securing all of the fruit slices. Bake the charm, following the clay manufacturer's instructions.

Fruit and cream earrings
The cream centre for these tarts is made by mixing white clay with a little liquid clay. Once you've added the fruit slices, use epoxy glue to fix the charms to earring posts.

Rainy-day cloud

Brighten up rainy days with this little stormy cloud, featuring colourful raindrops and a little bit of whimsy! Using a cutter you can create perfectly fluffy clouds easily and quickly, and with just a few simple steps, you will have as many clouds as you want!

1 Use a rolling pin to roll conditioned grey clay out to an even thickness of about 2 mm (¹⁄₁₆ in). Firmly press a 2 cm (³⁄₄ in) flower cutter all the way through the clay. Pull the cutter straight out. If the shape does not remain on the work surface, turn the cutter upside down and gently press at the edges on the wrong side of the shape until it drops out.

2 Use your fingers to smooth the edges of the cut shape, removing any rough or jagged areas left by the cutter.

3 Use a blade to cut straight across the flower, giving the cloud shape.

Skill level: ●●●

Actual size & dimensions

A Height 15 mm (⅝ in)
B Width 20 mm (¾ in)
C Depth 2 mm (¹⁄₁₆ in)

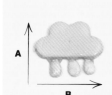

Weather brooch
These mini kilt pins make great little brooches. Why not team your rainy-day clouds with metal umbrella and cloud charms, or little crystal beads suggestive of raindrops?

Once baked the liquid clay will hold the droplet in place.

4 For the first raindrop, roll a teardrop shape in yellow clay, about 3 mm (⅛ in) long, then squash it flat with your finger until it is the same thickness as the grey cloud. Repeat to make a green and a pink raindrop.

5 Apply translucent liquid clay to the straight edge of the cloud then, using a cocktail stick, attach the first raindrop. Apply a little more liquid clay to the join. Fit the other two raindrops in place next to the first at the bottom of the rain cloud.

6 While the cloud and raindrops are still on the tile, carefully push an eyepin into the top of the cloud. Bake the cloud, following the clay manufacturer's instructions.

What's the forecast?
By changing the colour of the raindrops you can evoke different moods and weather conditions. Which is right for you?

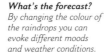

Fairy-tale acorn

Colour choice gives this acorn its unusual, unique appeal. More likely to be found in a fairy tale than on a forest floor, it could easily be paired with an enchanted mushroom (see pages 42–43). Experiment with colour ideas to create a cute bracelet for a little girl.

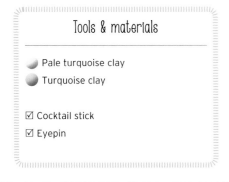

Join the flat edges of each shape.

1 Roll a marble-sized ball of conditioned pale turquoise clay between your hands. Gently press the ball onto the work surface to flatten one side.

2 Roll a marble-sized ball of conditioned turquoise clay, this time making the shape slightly longer than the pale turquoise ball. Press the clay against the work surface to flatten one side. Place the flat sides of each shape together and press gently to secure.

3 Roll several small balls of pale turquoise clay, about 1 mm (¹⁄₃₂ in) round, and place them all over the acorn's shell.

Skill level: ⬤⬤⬤

Actual size & dimensions

A Height 15 mm (⁵/₈ in)
B Width 10 mm (³/₈ in)
C Depth 10 mm (³/₈ in)

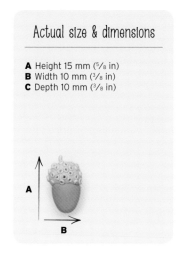

As an alternative to adding small dots of clay, use a cocktail stick to make holes directly through the acorn's cap.

Simply charming
Two different-coloured acorns sit happily together with two silver acorn charms on this simple necklace.

Take care to press into the centre of the ball each time.

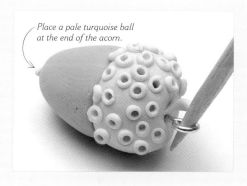

Place a pale turquoise ball at the end of the acorn.

4 Carefully press a cocktail stick into the centre of each ball, which will indent them and help fix them in place.

5 Use the cocktail stick to press one pale turquoise ball onto the end of the acorn. Roll a small snake of pale turquoise clay to act as the stem, and press it firmly in position on the end of the shell.

6 Use the cocktail stick to insert an eyepin through behind the acorn's stem, where it will be mostly hidden. Follow the clay manufacturer's instructions to bake the charm.

Nature's way
A turquoise acorn is a pretty and fanciful creation, but if you are looking for realism, use brown clays for your acorn. An oak leaf makes a fitting accompaniment.

Use an oak leaf cutter on green clay.

Mark veining lines with a needle.

Enchanted mushroom

When wandering in the woodland, what's more enchanting than stumbling across a fairy ring? Those charming little mushrooms work perfectly in charm form, especially in different shapes and sizes. The elements of the toadstool are easily moulded between your fingers, making this an easy charm to put together, and one that is perfect year-round for that little touch of magic.

Tools and materials

- ● Purple clay
- ● Orange clay

- ☑ Cocktail stick
- ☑ Eyepin

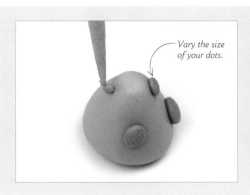

Vary the size of your dots.

1 Roll a small ball of conditioned purple clay about 5 mm (³/₁₆ in) wide. Slightly elongate the shape to form the mushroom's stalk.

2 Make a larger ball of conditioned orange clay and shape it to be more pointed at the top and flat at the bottom, like a cone.

3 Roll small dots of purple clay and use a cocktail stick to position them on the cap of the mushroom. Add both large and smaller dots for visual variety.

Cap in hand
Simple ways to vary the shape of your mushroom charms include making the cap flatter or more pointed, and the stalk longer or stumpier.

Skill level:

Actual size & dimensions

A Height 15 mm (⁵/₈ in)
B Width 10 mm (³/₈ in)
C Depth 10 mm (³/₈ in)

Creative collection
Add a collection of coloured fantasy mushrooms to a bracelet with silver toadstool charms in between.

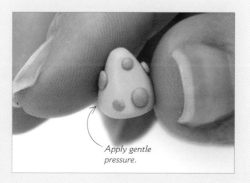

Apply gentle pressure.

4 With all of the dots in place, gently roll the mushroom top between your thumb and pointer finger to secure the dots.

5 Place the mushroom cap on top of the stalk and press down gently to fix the two together, remembering that if you do not do this gently the action could distort the shape of your finished mushroom.

6 Use the cocktail stick to gently insert an eyepin into the top of the mushroom. Using the cocktail stick in this way allows you to use steady and even pressure, which makes the insertion easier and more successful. Bake the mushroom, following the clay manufacturer's instructions.

TIP

Make sure your eyepin is long enough to go through the cap and partway into the stalk. This gives the mushroom extra strength and makes the elements less likely to separate.

Classic rose

Realistic little roses are the perfect addition to any bracelet, adding a feminine touch and a vintage feel. Delicate roses made with individual petals are not nearly as complex to make as they look. They use a simple technique and are quick and rewarding to make.

Tools & materials

● Purple clay

☑ Blade
☑ Cocktail stick
☑ Eyepin

Actual size & dimensions

A Height 18 mm (²³/₃₂ in)
B Width 18 mm (²³/₃₂ in)
C Depth 5 mm (³/₁₆ in)

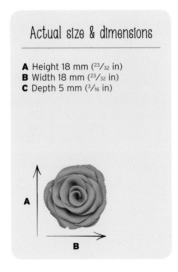

1 Start by rolling a selection of balls ranging in size from small, 2 mm (¹/₁₆ in), to large, 6 mm (¹/₄ in). Make sure the clay is well conditioned and soft to handle. For the rose to look natural you need to use balls of different sizes.

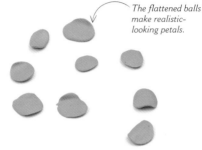

The flattened balls make realistic-looking petals.

2 Use a finger to flatten each ball onto the work surface. These shapes will form the petals. It is likely that the shapes will stick to the work surface so, to release them, gently press down onto the tile with a blade and scrape under the petals to lift them up.

3 Pick up one of the flattened petals and roll it between your fingers from one side to the next. Don't do this too tightly, otherwise you will not be able to see the spiral inside. If it is difficult to see the spiral, use one of your fingers to fan open the ends of the shape.

Start with the smallest petals, then build up the rose with larger petals in the next steps.

4 Continue to place petals around the outside of the first rolled-up petal. Place the new petals on alternating sides of the centre to build up an even coverage of petals.

Keep adding petals until you are happy with the shape of your rose.

5 Place more petals around the outside until you are happy with the shape of your rose. Try to keep all petals at a similar height so that the centre of the flower is level with the outside petals.

6 At the back of the rose there will be an excess of clay that needs to be removed. Pinch the back and roll it between your fingers until the clay is drawn away from the back of the flower. Then use a blade to trim the clay so that the back of the flower is flat.

Choose carefully
You could choose a colour for your rose based on the message you want to convey. A purple rose traditionally represents love at first sight, while the red rose is a well-known symbol of romantic love. A pink rose signifies first love, and a white rose indicates a secret admirer.

TIP

The larger the balls of clay you roll in Step 1, the larger your flower will be. If you keep adding petals of the same size the rose will not look very realistic, which is why it is important to have a variety of different-sized balls. Try to use the smaller petals on the inside and the larger petals on the outside.

7 Use a cocktail stick to gently insert an eyepin into the rose just behind the final layer of petals. Bake the clay rose, following the manufacturer's instructions.

Singular simplicity
This intricate charm stands out beautifully on its own. Instead of adding an eyepin, use epoxy glue to attach a single rose to a flat-pad ring.

Flower posy

This little cluster of flowers makes a wonderful charm for a pendant or earring set, and is a fabulous idea for wedding jewellery. The mini bouquet is formed using individual flowers. It is a time-consuming project, but it achieves a beautiful result.

Tools and materials

- Purple clay
- Yellow clay
- Pink clay
- Lilac clay
- Translucent liquid clay

☑ Cocktail stick
☑ Eyepin

Actual size & dimensions

A Height 15 mm (⁵⁄₈ in)
B Width 15 mm (⁵⁄₈ in)
C Depth 10 mm (³⁄₈ in)

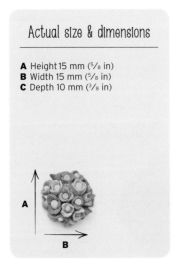

1 Start by rolling balls of conditioned clay about 2 mm (¹⁄₁₆ in) round, three in purple and one yellow. These balls will be used to form one flower.

2 Use a finger to squash the purple balls into flat disks that will form the petals. The yellow ball is the flower's centre.

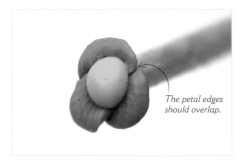

The petal edges should overlap.

3 Place the yellow ball on the end of a cocktail stick. Carefully pick up one petal at a time and wrap it around the centre. Overlap the petals slightly so that they look natural.

4 Repeat Steps 1–3 to make at least 20 flowers, some with purple, some with pink and some with lilac petals. Bake the flowers for five minutes so that they can be handled without misshaping.

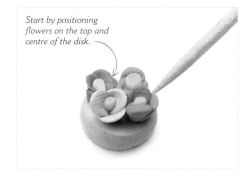

Start by positioning flowers on the top and centre of the disk.

5 Flatten some conditioned lilac clay into a disk about 1 cm (³⁄₈ in) in diameter and 5 mm (³⁄₁₆ in) thick.

6 Apply small amounts of translucent liquid clay to the lilac disk and place the baked flowers on top. Push down firmly with the cocktail stick to ensure that the flowers are well attached.

Classic pendant
Team your posy with a small metal leaf charm on a simple pendant necklace that really shows off the beauty of this charm.

Secure the flowers with a little extra liquid clay before baking.

7 Repeat Step 6 until the base is covered with the flowers. Use the cocktail stick to insert an eyepin between the flowers and the side of the charm.

8 To ensure that none of the flowers become detached from the base, apply liquid clay into the gaps between them, using a cocktail stick for easy and accurate application. Bake the whole charm, following the clay manufacturer's instructions.

Ring idea
For an alternative, leave out the eyepin and use epoxy glue to fix the posy to a flat-pad finding such as this ring, for a beautiful floral accessory.

Bird's nest

This adorable little bird's nest will make you tweet with delight! Although this project can get a little tricky, and you need some specific tools, it's so worth it. The attention to detail is what really makes this charm.

Tools & materials

● Tan clay
● Blue clay
● Green clay

☑ Extruder with 1 mm (¹/₃₂ in) multiple string plate
☑ Rolling pin
☑ 1.5 cm (⁵/₈ in) round cutter
☑ Blade
☑ Cocktail stick
☑ Eyepin
☑ Black permanent marker

Actual size & dimensions

A Height 20 mm (³/₄ in)
B Width 20 mm (³/₄ in)
C Depth 3 mm (¹/₈ in)

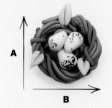

Make sure the clay is very soft for easier extrusion.

1 Roll a ball of tan clay slightly larger than a marble between your hands until it is really soft. Put the ball into an extruder fitted with a 1 mm (¹/₃₂ in) multiple string plate. Extrude the clay until it has all been pushed out.

2 Twist the extruded clay strands together. These should look like branches and twigs, and will form the sides of the nest.

TIP

If you don't have an extruder, don't panic! You can always roll the thin strands by hand. Gently roll the clay on a work surface until it is long and thin. The strands may not be of such an even thickness, but that will just add to the wild look!

3 Use a rolling pin to roll out some more tan clay to a thickness of about 1 mm (¹/₃₂ in) and use a 1.5 cm (⁵/₈ in) round cutter to cut out a disk. This will form the base of the nest.

In the trees
Team the bird's nest with silver leaf charms on either side on a mini safety pin, to complete the natural theme.

The join will be hidden in a later step, so don't worry about how it looks now.

Varied egg sizes will look more natural.

4 Wrap the snake of twisted strands around the base disk by securing it at the starting point then working your way around, pressing gently until you are back where you started. Use a blade to cut off the extra clay.

5 Make a small spiral from a little of the leftover clay and use a cocktail stick to position this in the bottom of the nest: this will help position the eggs later, and ensures that the nest does not look unnaturally flat.

6 Roll three small egg shapes from blue clay, about 3 mm (⅛ in) long and 2 mm (¹⁄₁₆ in) wide. Varying the shape and size slightly will give the eggs a more realistic appearance.

Manoeuvre the eggs with a cocktail stick so you don't distort their shape.

7 Carefully place the eggs in the nest, facing in different directions and at different angles so they do not look too organized. Use the cocktail stick to gently move them around so you do not crush them with your fingers.

8 Make three little leaves (see page 133) from green clay, about 3 mm (⅛ in) long. Use one of these to cover the join in the tan clay, pressing it down gently to fix it in place. Place the other leaves around the edge of the nest.

9 Insert an eyepin into the base of the nest and bake following the clay manufacturer's instructions. Once baked and cooled, make dots on the eggs with a permanent marker to give them that perfect natural look!

Scandinavian birdhouse

With its cute door, heart-shaped window and matching roof tiles, what bird wouldn't call this little house their home? Team this charm with some folk-style birds (see pages 60-61) to complete the theme.

Tools & materials

- Peach clay
- Blue clay
- Turquoise clay

- ☑ Rolling pin
- ☑ 1.5 cm (⅝ in) oval cutter
- ☑ Blade
- ☑ Cocktail stick
- ☑ Eyepin

Actual size & dimensions

A Height 20 mm (¾ in)
B Width 12.5 mm (½ in)
C Depth 3 mm (⅛ in)

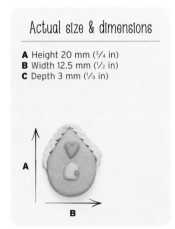

1 Use a rolling pin to roll conditioned peach clay to a thickness of about 3 mm (⅛ in). Gently press a 1.5 cm (⅝ in) oval cutter through the clay. Remove the cutter and excess surrounding clay, leaving the shape.

2 Use a blade to slice off the rounded edges at the top of the house to create the steep angle of the roof. Aim to press firmly into the clay, rather than dragging the blade through.

3 Roll out a long, thin sheet of blue clay, about 1 mm (¹⁄₃₂ in) thick.

Leave the slices on the blade.

4 Use the blade to cut slices from the sheet of blue clay for the roof tiles. Let the slices stack up on the blade, to help ensure you have equally sized tiles and to make positioning them on the roof easier.

Birdhouse bracelet
Team your birdhouses with coordinating coloured beads. Added silver birdhouses and swallows give this bracelet a vintage feel.

For the sake of aesthetics, make sure each side of the roof features the same number of tiles.

A few straight lines give the effect of wood grain.

5 Once you have enough slices on the blade to cover one side of the angled roof edge, transfer the tiles to the roof line. Repeat Steps 4-5 for the other roof slant.

6 Make a little front door by pushing a ball of blue clay onto the surface of the house. Use the blade to texture the door to resemble wood grain. Add a tiny dot of turquoise clay as a door handle.

Perfect little homes
Vary the basic body shape or colours to create similar little houses. A clock face turns a birdhouse into a cuckoo clock.

7 Make a turquoise heart shape, about 3 mm (⅛ in) in length, and gently press it into position above the door.

8 Use a cocktail stick to slowly and carefully insert an eyepin into the charm through the apex of the roof. Bake the clay charm, following the manufacturer's instructions.

Mix liquid clay with pink clay and paint on the hearts. Make the hands from black clay.

Potted cactus

These cute little cacti make perfect prickly accessories to your charm bracelet. Using a variety of different styles and colour combinations you can build up a collection of endearing plants with thorns, flowers and different-shaped plant pots. Let your imagination run wild.

Actual size & dimensions

A Length 15 mm (⁵/₈ in)
B Width 7.5 mm (⁵/₁₆ in)
C Depth 5 mm (³/₁₆ in)

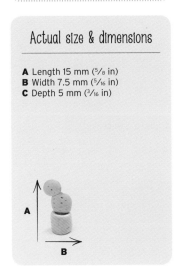

1 To make a small cylinder of grey clay for the pot, about 1 cm (³/₈ in) long and 5 mm (³/₁₆ in) wide, start by rolling a thick log of conditioned clay. Use a blade to cut off both curved ends, creating a flat top and bottom.

2 To make the soil in the pot, roll a tiny ball of conditioned brown clay, about 2 mm (¹/₁₆ in) wide. Press the ball onto the top of the plant pot and push down gently to flatten it.

3 Make two pea-sized balls of green clay and use your finger to flatten one of the balls to form a disk shape. Roll the other ball into a log and slightly flatten it, ensuring that it does not appear completely two-dimensional.

Apply only a small amount of liquid clay.

4 Place the two green shapes together and use translucent liquid clay to secure. Liquid clay can make the objects slippery when too much is applied, so use it carefully, and press together gently.

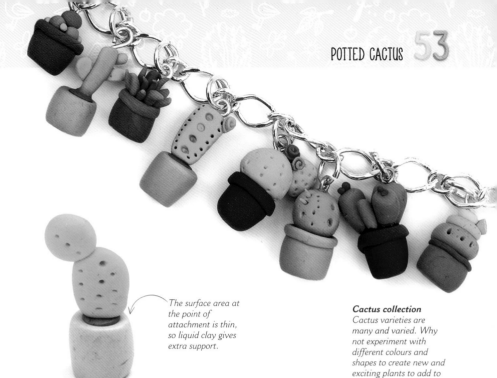

Cactus collection
Cactus varieties are many and varied. Why not experiment with different colours and shapes to create new and exciting plants to add to your charm collection?

The surface area at the point of attachment is thin, so liquid clay gives extra support.

5 Press a cocktail stick into the surface of the clay to texture it and suggest the plant's spiky appearance.

6 Now carefully lift the cactus plant onto the plant pot and use liquid clay to hold it in place, once again pressing down carefully to join the two items while not disturbing the shapes created.

7 Use the cocktail stick to help insert an eyepin straight down into the centre of the charm. Bake the charm, following the clay manufacturer's instructions.

Roll a snake and flatten it on the work surface to make a lip for a pot.

Potted inspiration
Mix up your pots as well as your plants, using different clay colours and adjusting the basic shape.

Roll balls of clay on the work surface until they resemble spikes, and group them together on an aloe vera plant.

Spiral one tiny rose petal (see Step 3, page 44) to make a flower.

Bake the spikes before attaching them with a little liquid clay.

Pine tree

Individually moulding the needles for this pine-tree charm may be time-consuming, but that extra touch is what gives the tree its depth and texture. Once you have mastered this tree, think about other ways you can recreate natural foliage effects.

Tools & materials

● Brown clay
● Green clay

☑ Cocktail stick
☑ Eyepin
☑ Black permanent marker

Actual size & dimensions

A Height 20 mm (³⁄₄ in)
B Width 8 mm (⁵⁄₁₆ in)
C Depth 8 mm (⁵⁄₁₆ in)

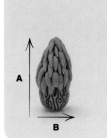

1 Roll conditioned brown clay into a ball and flatten each end against your work surface to form the shape of a tree trunk, about 6 mm (¹⁄₄ in) in height and width.

Make the foliage element of the tree twice as tall as the trunk.

2 Make the main body of the tree by forming a cone shape from conditioned green clay, twice the height of the trunk and slightly wider.

Press together gently to avoid distorting either shape.

3 Place the green cone on the brown trunk and gently press the two together.

4 Make small green cone shapes, about 2 mm (¹⁄₁₆ in) long, for the pine needles. You will need quite a few!

Skill level: ● ● ●

Use a pair of scissors to snip into the clay to give a spiky appearance. Do not snip too deeply, otherwise the charm will fall apart.

A woodland walk
Combine these miniature tree charms with other woodland charms for a nature-inspired bracelet that is perfect for any outdoorsy person.

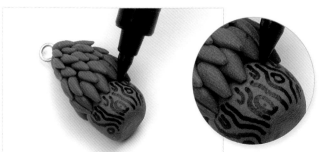

Each row of pine needles overlaps the row below, with the points sitting in the gaps.

Using small balls of clay as leaves gives a different type of tree.

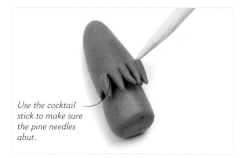

Use the cocktail stick to make sure the pine needles abut.

5 Starting at the base of the green cone, use a cocktail stick to position a line of pine needles around the tree. Make sure they sit close together. When this first row is complete, use your finger to gently press the pine needles down.

6 Position a second row of pine needles above the first, ensuring that the pine needles sit in between the ones below, overlapping slightly. Continue adding rows of pine needles, pressing each section down securely before moving on to the next.

7 Use the cocktail stick to insert an eyepin into the top of the tree, making sure the pin goes in straight. Follow the clay manufacturer's instructions to bake the charm.

8 Let the baked charm cool, then use black permanent marker to draw bark markings on the tree's trunk.

Winter pine
For a snow-dusted look, paint white modelling material onto the tips of the baked foliage.

Hot-air balloon

Up! Up! And away! There is something mesmerizing and graceful about hot-air balloons, and these lovable miniatures are so realistic you'll wish you could hop aboard and fly away. With a few delicate steps, these balloons are tricky to make but well worth the effort.

Tools & materials

- Magenta clay
- Turquoise clay
- Lilac clay
- Green clay
- Brown clay

- ☑ Blade
- ☑ Cocktail stick
- ☑ Eyepin

Actual size & dimensions

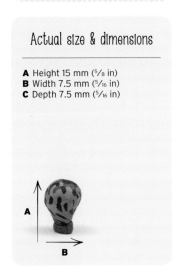

A Height 15 mm (⅝ in)
B Width 7.5 mm (⁵⁄₁₆ in)
C Depth 7.5 mm (⁵⁄₁₆ in)

1 Start by rolling a selection of snakes of conditioned clay in lilac, turquoise, magenta and green, each about 5 cm (2 in) long and 1 mm (¹⁄₃₂ in) thick. These will form the cane that will make up the pattern on the balloon.

Pile the shapes together in a random order.

2 Place all of the snakes together to form one cane and roll gently on the work surface to eliminate any air bubbles. Use a blade to cut the cane in half.

3 Place the two halves together again to make a wider cane. Roll together gently.

4 Use the blade to cut thin slices from the end of the cane. The thinner the slices the further the clay will go, allowing you to cover more of the balloon.

Skill level: ●●●

The sky's the limit
The wearer of this bracelet will need to try hard not to keep their head in the clouds. Hot-air balloons are teamed perfectly with metal weather-inspired charms.

Keep rolling the covered ball between your hands until you can no longer see the joins.

Make horizontal and vertical marks with the blade.

5 Roll a ball of conditioned magenta clay about 5 mm (³⁄₁₆ in) wide. Wrap the slices from the cane around the outside of the ball, trying to ensure that the majority of the ball is covered. Roll this ball gently between your hands to force the slices to merge together and create a seamless ball.

6 Pinch the bottom of the sphere and roll this between two fingers to mould the iconic balloon shape.

7 Roll a small cylinder of conditioned brown clay about 5 mm (³⁄₁₆ in) long and 3 mm (¹⁄₈ in) wide. This will form the balloon's basket. Use the blade to texture the basket so that it looks woven.

The eyepin will hold the basket and balloon together securely.

8 Place the balloon onto the basket and gently press the two together, taking care not to distort either shape.

9 Using a cocktail stick, gently insert an eyepin into the top of the balloon. Bake the charm, following the clay manufacturer's instructions.

Balloon fiesta
The cane rolling technique allows you to cover any number of balloons in a huge range of colour combinations. You can also adjust the shape of your balloon, and create your own little fleet of hot-air balloons!

Butterfly wings

This surprisingly simple technique produces intricate results that suggest a great deal of skill has been used. The natural-looking pattern is made by combining and extruding clay, while a little pinching and smoothing creates the wing shape. As an added bonus, this method of making means you can easily produce a number of wing charms in one shot.

Tools & materials

- Orange clay
- Brown clay
- Black clay

- ☑ Rolling pin
- ☑ Extruder with rectangle plate
- ☑ Blade
- ☑ Cocktail stick

Actual size & dimensions

A Height 25 mm (1 in)
B Width 15 mm (⁵⁄₈ in)
C Depth 3 mm (¹⁄₈ in)

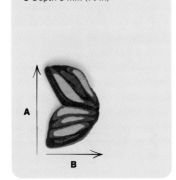

1 Thoroughly condition the orange clay in your hands until it is really soft and pliable. Roll the clay into a log about 2.5 cm (1 in) long and 1 cm (³⁄₈ in) wide.

2 Use a rolling pin to roll out a sheet of conditioned brown clay to about 3 mm (¹⁄₈ in) thick. Wrap the brown sheet around the orange log.

Messy ends don't matter.

3 Repeat Step 2 with black clay. Don't worry if the ends look untidy at this stage.

4 Place the cane inside an extruder with a rectangle plate and turn the handle until all of the clay has been pushed through.

Skill level: ● ● ●

Wing chain
To attach this charm to a bracelet, simply thread a jump ring through the hole made in Step 8.

5 Use a blade to cut the extruded cane into four sections of equal length. Stack these on top of each other in any order.

Smooth here.

Pinch here.

6 Start to mould the stack into half of a butterfly wing shape by pinching one side with your fingers while smoothing out the other side until rounded.

Pinch the ends together.

7 Cut the shaped stack in half and place the two points together to complete the wing shape. Secure the join by pressing gently.

8 Use the blade to cut the stack into thin wings, about 3 mm (⅛ in) thick. Press down slowly and evenly to avoid misshaping the clay. Use a cocktail stick to make a hole in the top corner of each wing. Bake the wings, following the clay manufacturer's instructions.

Make a Skinner blend (see page 129) and shape the clay into a cube, then into a wing shape. Wrap the shape and cut into three pieces, then stack, cut and shape again to create four wing elements.

A snake of pink clay wrapped with green clay has been stretched, stacked and cut to produce this wing pattern.

Wing things
Experiment with cutting and stacking techniques to create various patterns.

Folk-style bird

This folk bird charm, inspired by Scandinavian style and traditional patterns, uses bold colours in combination with patterning and texturing techniques that, once mastered, are easy to reuse for other charms. The birds can be interpreted in many different shapes and styles, so let your imagination go wild!

Tools & materials

- Pastel green clay
- Magenta clay
- Purple clay
- Orange clay

- ☑ Cocktail stick
- ☑ Blade
- ☑ Eyepin

Actual size & dimensions

A Height 12.5 mm (½ in)
B Width 25 mm (1 in)
C Depth 5 mm (³⁄₁₆ in)

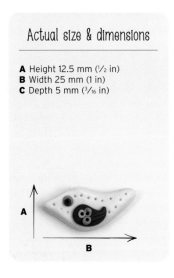

1 Start by making a marble-sized ball of conditioned pastel green clay. This will be shaped into the bird's body by moulding with the fingers.

Mould the clay with your fingers until you are happy with your bird's body shape.

2 Hold the ball between your fingers and pinch the beak and tail shape away from the centre of the ball, and pull slightly. When the shape resembles the one shown here, slightly flatten the clay until it is about 5 mm (³⁄₁₆ in) deep.

3 Take a small ball of conditioned magenta clay and pull one end into a point to form a teardrop shape about 5 mm (³⁄₁₆ in) long. Shape this into a wing and flatten using a finger. Place the wing on the bird's body.

4 Roll two small dots of purple clay and one of orange clay. Position the orange dot at the top of the wing and the purple dots next to it. Secure the shapes by pressing a cocktail stick into the centre of each one.

Skill level: ●●●

Button and bird
Create a pendant for a necklace by attaching charms and beads to one large jump ring, so that the necklace will hang evenly. Adding a coordinating button means the necklace is not too bulky.

5 Form the bird's eye by placing a magenta dot of clay on top of a slightly larger purple ball of clay, then press the two down with the cocktail stick.

6 Add feather detailing to the wing by gently pressing a blade into the pointed end of the teardrop shape to make linear indents.

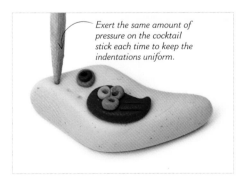

Exert the same amount of pressure on the cocktail stick each time to keep the indentations uniform.

7 Add texture to the bird's body by gently pressing the point of the cocktail stick into the surface of the clay to create dimples.

8 Use the cocktail stick to carefully insert an eyepin into the bird's body so that it will hang straight. Bake the charm, following the clay manufacturer's instructions.

It is very easy to mould the initial ball of clay into slightly different shapes for the bird's body.

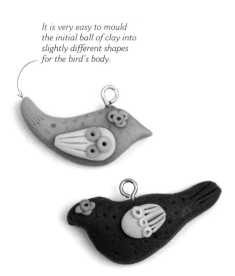

Feathered friends
Vary the clay colours and pattern placement to create a limitless supply of folk birds.

Tools and materials

- 🟣 Mauve clay
- 🟣 Purple clay
- 🔵 Pastel blue clay
- 🔵 Blue clay
- 🔵 Turquoise clay

- ☑ Cocktail stick
- ☑ Eyepin
- ☑ Black permanent marker

Tiny owl

Everyone's favourite nocturnal bird is napping again! This sleepy little fellow would look wonderful on a bird-themed bracelet, perhaps with the parrot from pages 64-65, or even with other wildlife, like the little deer on pages 68-69.

Use the cocktail stick to nudge the beak into position.

1 Roll a small amount of conditioned mauve clay between your hands into an oblong shape, about 1.5 cm (⁵⁄₈ in) long and 5 mm (³⁄₁₆ in) wide. Try to make the shape slightly narrower at the top than at the bottom. Use your fingers to roll two small purple teardrops, about 3 mm (⅛ in) long. Place the teardrops on either side of the body at the same height, for the wings. Gently press the wings on with a cocktail stick, then carefully lift the bottom of each one so that it flicks upward.

2 Make the eyes by rolling two balls of conditioned pastel blue clay and flattening them. Together they should be roughly the same width as the top part of the owl's body. Position them on the owl between the wings. Roll two snakes of blue clay just under 1 cm (³⁄₈ in) long. These will form the owl's feather eyebrows. Using the cocktail stick, place one end of one snake in between the eyes, then wrap it around the top of one eye and flick the other end up. Repeat for the other eyebrow.

3 Make a purple heart shape, about 3 mm (⅛ in) long, for the beak, and place it just below and between the eyes.

Skill level: ● ● ●

Actual size & dimensions

A Height 15 mm (⁵⁄₈ in)
B Width 20 mm (³⁄₄ in)
C Depth 7.5 mm (⁵⁄₁₆ in)

Wakey wakey
To make a version that's awake, once the charm is baked simply draw on some big beautiful eyes, eyelashes and all!

A simple drawn-on motif finishes off the sleepy owl character.

4 Roll three small dots of turquoise clay, about 1 mm (¹⁄₃₂ in) round, and place them across the stomach of the owl, one in the centre and one on either side. Press the cocktail stick into the centre of each dot to secure it in place.

5 Carefully insert an eyepin into the top of the owl, using the cocktail stick to slowly guide it in. Now bake the charm, following the clay manufacturer's instructions, and leave to cool.

6 When the owl is cool, draw on his eyes. Use black permanent marker to draw a curved line, then draw small lines coming away from that line as the eyelashes.

Family tree
Now that you have the basics down, try making different owls by altering the base shape and adjusting the details.

Instead of drawing eyes, you could mould them from clay disks and circles.

Pinch ears out of the egg-shaped body.

Peachy parrot

The colours used here resemble those of the salmon-crested cockatoo, which has a reputation for being difficult and noisy. This little bird takes time to make, but is easy to keep, and you won't hear a peep out of him!

Tools & materials

- Peach clay
- Bright pink clay
- Pink clay
- White clay

- ☑ Cocktail stick
- ☑ Rolling pin
- ☑ Eyepin
- ☑ Black permanent marker

Actual size & dimensions

A Height 15 mm (⅝ in)
B Width 35 mm (1 ⅜ in)
C Depth 10 mm (⅜ in)

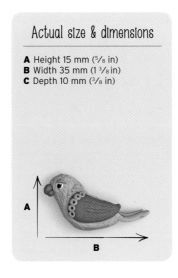

Pull the point through the surface of the clay several times.

1 Roll a marble-sized ball of conditioned peach clay between your hands. Use your hand to flatten the ball, then pinch each end until the clay resembles the shape shown, and is about 2 cm (¾ in) long.

2 To create the featherlike texture, gently drag a cocktail stick along the surface of the clay, trying not to go too deep.

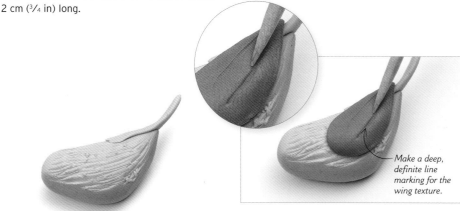

Make a deep, definite line marking for the wing texture.

3 Use a rolling pin to roll a thin, flat oval shape of peach clay for the tail. Position this at the back end of the bird so that roughly half of the shape sits on its body, with the rest coming off the end as the tail.

4 Shape a large bright pink teardrop for the wing; this should take up the space of about half the body. Use the cocktail stick to texture this with a few lines that are deeper and wider than the body texturing.

Skill level:

Keep it simple
Place this detailed and textured parrot with a more simple charm, so as not to detract from it.

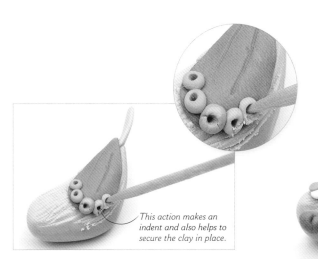

This action makes an indent and also helps to secure the clay in place.

5 Roll small dots of pink clay, about 2 mm (1/16 in) round, and position a line of these around the curve of the wing. Press the cocktail stick into the centre of each ball.

6 For the beak, make two small, bright pink teardrop shapes and press them together, then place in position. Roll a small ball of white clay and place in position as an eye, then position a pink ball above it for the eyelid.

If you want to, add more feather texture to the bird's body before baking.

7 Add a strip of pink clay to the tail, then use the cocktail stick to insert an eyepin through the parrot's head.

8 Bake the clay, following the manufacturer's instructions. Allow the charm to cool, then use black permanent marker to draw the pupil onto the white eye.

Bold birds
Use the same techniques but brighter colours to replicate vibrant macaws.

You can use a ball of white clay for a highlight in the eye.

Add some sparkle with red glitter clay for the body and metallic gold for the wings and beak.

Pampered poodle

This pretty little girl is groomed to perfection, with her characteristic curly ears and a pretty bow to complete the look. If you are planning on making a dog charm to represent a real pet, think about that animal's personality traits, and try to replicate them in the charm.

Tools & materials

- Mauve clay
- Pink clay
- Black clay

- ☑ Rolling pin
- ☑ Cocktail stick
- ☑ Eyepin
- ☑ Black permanent marker

Actual size & dimensions

A Height 12.5 mm (¹/₂ in)
B Width 25 mm (1 in)
C Depth 10 mm (³/₈ in) at the widest point

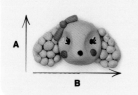

1 Roll a ball of conditioned mauve clay, about the size of a marble. Use your hands to smooth it all over and eliminate any cracks.

Use one finger to press each eye indent.

2 Gently press down into the ball with one finger to create each eye shape, then pinch the nose out from the centre.

3 Use a rolling pin to roll mauve clay to a thickness of 1 mm (¹/₃₂ in). Form the sheet into two teardrop shapes 1.5 cm (⁵/₈ in) long. Place these under the poodle's head as ears, and press gently into position.

The balls don't need to be exactly the same size, but make sure they don't vary wildly.

4 Roll a number of mauve balls, all roughly 2 mm (¹/₁₆ in) across. Use a cocktail stick to press these balls in place on the poodle's ears, until they are completely covered.

French poodle
Attach this little lady to a jump ring to create a pendant for a necklace. A large charm like this one does not need to be teamed with other pieces, although an Eiffel Tower charm would make a fitting accompaniment in this case.

5 Roll two pink dots and press in place for the poodle's cheeks. Roll a smaller black dot and place this on the end of the nose.

6 Make a bow using pink clay by rolling one small ball and two small teardrop shapes. Position the bow on the poodle's head and press down gently.

Handbag poodle
While a real pet is not an accessory, this charm version is cute and harmless. Mould the bag shape to your liking, then slice into the top and open it out. Add your decoration and a ball of clay inside the bag. Make a smaller pampered poodle so that 2 mm (¹⁄₁₆ in) of the eyepin sticks out at the bottom, and insert this into the clay ball to secure the whole charm.

7 Using the cocktail stick to keep it level, insert an eyepin into the top of the poodle's head. Bake the charm, following the clay manufacturer's instructions.

8 Let the charm cool after baking, then use a black permanent marker to draw in the poodle's eyes.

Roll out a thin sheet of silver clay and cut out tiny rectangles for the zipper.

Tools & materials

- Pastel pink clay
- Grey clay
- White clay
- Pink clay

- ☑ Blade
- ☑ Eyepin
- ☑ Cocktail stick
- ☑ White acrylic paint
- ☑ Paintbrush
- ☑ Black permanent marker

Dear deer

This lovable little deer would look charming on a necklace, or make an adorable addition to a forest-themed bracelet, perhaps with a mushroom or two (see pages 42–43). Modeling and painting techniques are used to form a base for the head, which is carefully finished off with a little clay and pen detailing.

1 Roll a ball of conditioned pastel pink clay about the size of a marble for the deer's head. Slightly flatten one edge of the ball so that it will stand without rolling, to make the moulding stages easier. Start to shape the head by pinching the nose out and upward.

2 Pinch out two ears at the top of the head. These should be placed evenly on each side, and the clay should not be made too thin, no less than 1 mm (¹⁄₃₂ in). Shape the ears to make them pointed and use your fingers to make dents for the eyes and indents in the ears. If you feel confident enough, use a blade to neaten the shape and make sharp outlines around the ears.

3 Insert an eyepin between the ears, using a cocktail stick to ensure good placement and to avoid distorting the shape. Bake the head for five minutes so that the clay is no longer soft and will not change shape during painting.

Skill level: ● ● ●

Actual size & dimensions

A Height 15 mm (⁵⁄₈ in)
B Width 20 mm (³⁄₄ in)
C Depth 10 mm (³⁄₈ in)

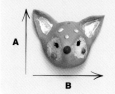

Ball-chain necklace
This cute and intricate charm does not need to be surrounded with other charms; it has impact on its own.

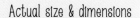

Dot the white paint into the indents of the ears and cheeks.

Use the cocktail stick to help position the tiny balls of clay.

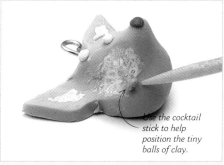

4 Use a paintbrush to dot white acrylic paint onto the ears, on the cheeks and where the eyes will be. The paint provides a surface to work onto with the permanent marker, and ensures that detailing will be visible.

Doe eyes
This variation shows how you can use clay instead of paint and pen for some of the detailing. White clay on top of black clay makes a nice highlight for the eyes.

Instead of paint, use flesh light clay for the inside of the ear, pressed into shape with a ball tool.

5 Roll one grey ball, three white balls and two pink balls, each about 1 mm (¹⁄₃₂ in) round. Place the grey ball on the end of the nose and the three white balls in a triangle on the forehead. Place a pink ball on each cheek, quite low so that there is still plenty of room for the eyes. Firmly press down the balls so that they are attached well to the head.

6 Bake the head fully, following the clay manufacturer's instructions. When the charm is cool, use a black permanent marker to carefully draw eyes with little eyelashes, ensuring both sides are the same and even.

Tools & materials

- ⚪ White clay
- ⚫ Black clay
- ⚪ Pink clay
- ⚪ Bright green clay
- ⚫ Dark green clay

- ☑ Cocktail stick
- ☑ Eyepin
- ☑ Black permanent marker

Hungry panda

Bamboo contains little nutritional value, so pandas need to eat a lot of it to meet their energy needs, which is why this hungry chap is carefully clinging onto his bamboo snack. Creating and positioning all the little parts of this charm are what makes it an intermediate project, but the result is so endearing that you'll want to put the effort in.

Make sure the cheeks are level.

1 Roll a ball of conditioned white clay about the size of a marble. Once the ball is smooth, shape it with your hands so that it is longer and more egg shaped. Form two small balls from conditioned black clay, about 2 mm (1/16 in) round, and place them on top of the white shape as the panda's ears.

2 Roll a ball of black clay about 3 mm (1/8 in) round. Use your finger to press it flat, and position it on the white body where one eye will be. Roll two 1 mm (1/32 in) balls of pink clay for the panda's cheeks. Position one on each side of the panda's face.

3 Roll a small bright green string, about 5 mm (3/16 in) long and 1 mm (1/32 in) wide. Place it diagonally across the panda's chest. Form two tiny dark green teardrop shapes and position one on either side of the bright green branch.

Actual size & dimensions

A Height 15 mm (⁵⁄₈ in)
B Width 10 mm (³⁄₈ in)
C Depth 10 mm (³⁄₈ in)

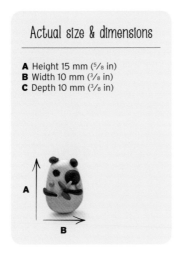

Panda and pom-pom
Team this little hungry panda with felt balls in coordinating colours that bring out his rosy cheeks and the green of the bamboo.

Let the black paw overlap the green branch to look like the panda is holding the snack.

4 Roll a small amount of black clay between your fingers to make two arms, each one about 5 mm (³⁄₁₆ in) long and 1 mm (¹⁄₃₂ in) wide. Position these on the panda's body, overlapping the branch slightly so that it looks like the panda is holding it.

5 Use a cocktail stick to insert an eyepin through the top of the charm, between the panda's ears.

6 Use your finger to indent the front of each ear and make them both stand up a little taller. Bake the charm, following the clay manufacturer's instructions. Let the charm cool, then use black permanent marker to draw three little lines for each of the panda's eyes.

Animal pals
Change the ears and facial features to make other animals, then add on the relevant accessories.

Mix liquid clay with gold and yellow clay to make the runny honey. Don't forget to add a drop to his paw.

Walking penguin

This darling little penguin is the perfect addition to your winter wardrobe, and is made using a combination of techniques both before and after baking. While he will fit into any charm collection, he would be especially at home on a winter-warmer bracelet with the gingerbread house, Christmas tree and festive stocking (see pages 110–115).

Curl up the wing tips to give the character a sense of movement.

1 Roll a ball of conditioned grey clay to about the size of a marble. Roll it gently between your palms to ensure a smooth and rounded appearance. Roll a ball of conditioned white clay and flatten it into a disk that is a little smaller than one side of your grey ball. Place the disk on the grey ball and smooth it down so that the two are flat against each other.

2 Make two grey teardrop shapes about 5 mm (³/₁₆ in) long and 3 mm (¹/₈ in) wide. These will form the penguin's wings. Press them onto the grey body on either side of the white circle. When the wings are secure, use a finger to curl the bottom of each one upward, to give the impression of flapping and waddling!

3 Make a small yellow heart for the beak, and use a cocktail stick to press this gently into position on the white circle just below centre.

You could try clay instead of pen for the eyes.

This smart guy's body is an egg shape, with an oval for the chest.

Use pearl grey clay for the body and wings.

Emperor penguin
The basics of this project can be altered slightly to make different penguin characters.

Actual size & dimensions

A Height 12 mm (¹⁵/₃₂ in)
B Width 20 mm (³/₄ in)
C Depth 10 mm (³/₈ in)

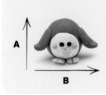

A

B

Two's company
Create a different style of penguin and place them side by side on a necklace chain. These happy little guys are always more at home when huddled together.

Take care with the angle at which you insert the eyepin, to ensure that the charm will hang straight.

All it takes is two dots to bring the little chap to life.

4 Insert an eyepin into the grey clay at the top of the penguin. Use the cocktail stick to guide the pin in smoothly and steadily, ensuring that it goes in straight and does not distort the shape of the charm.

5 Make two smaller yellow heart shapes for the feet. Sit the penguin on top of the shapes and press down gently so that the feet attach themselves on. Use the cocktail stick to lift the end of one foot up slightly to give the impression that the penguin is walking.

6 Roll two tiny dots of pastel pink clay, about 1 mm (¹/₃₂ in) wide, and place them either side of the beak. Bake the charm, following the clay manufacturer's instructions. When cool, use a black permanent marker to draw on two dots for eyes to give the penguin a charming little face.

Little blue whale

In a break from the norm, our blue whale is small and sweet, with a burst of water coming out from his blow hole. The techniques for making him can be easily adapted to other marine favourites, using natural or fanciful clay colours.

Actual size & dimensions

A Height 10 mm (³⁄₈ in)
B Width 15 mm (⁵⁄₈ in)
C Depth 10 mm (³⁄₈ in)

1 Roll a marble-sized ball of conditioned blue clay between your hands until smooth.

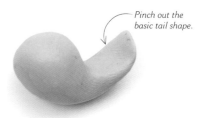

Pinch out the basic tail shape.

2 Pinch one side of the ball of clay to begin forming the whale's tail.

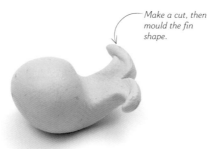

Make a cut, then mould the fin shape.

3 Use a blade to make a small cut in the end of the tail and curve these edges outward to form a fin.

4 Form a teardrop shape from conditioned pastel blue clay, smaller than the whale's body, and press your finger into it to flatten it. Press this onto the whale's side.

Skill level: ● ● ●

Narwhal brooch
If you prefer the rarer underwater mammal, why not make a narwhal? Twist two thin pieces of clay together into a horn and position it at the front of your whale's head.

5 Use a cocktail stick to make a small indent for the whale's blow hole. Form two tiny dark blue teardrop shapes and use the cocktail stick to press these into the blow hole.

6 Roll a tiny pink ball and press this onto the whale's cheek, beside the pastel blue fin.

The hand-drawn eye adds the finishing touch.

Changing shape
Elongate the original whale body shape to create a slimline dolphin. Make sure the teardrop fin is also lengthened to match the body shape.

7 Use the cocktail stick to help position an eyepin just behind the blow hole. Bake the clay, following the manufacturer's instructions.

8 Allow the charm to cool after baking, then use black permanent marker to draw on the whale's eye, and maybe a few eyelashes!

A mix of blue, grey and silver clay has been used for the dolphin's body.

Use a needle to indent the mouth.

Vintage teapot

This vintage-inspired teapot makes a great addition to any charm bracelet. The tea-party craze is at an all-time high, so why not celebrate with an afternoon-tea bracelet? You could team this teapot charm with miniature cupcakes (see pages 18-19) and fruit-tart charms (see pages 36-37) to make a gorgeous accessory.

Tools & materials

- Purple clay
- Green clay
- Pale purple clay
- Pink clay
- Translucent liquid clay

☑ Pin
☑ Eyepin
☑ Cocktail stick

Actual size & dimensions

A Height 15 mm (⅝ in)
B Width 20 mm (¾ in)
C Depth 5 mm (³⁄₁₆ in)

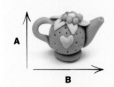

Press down very gently so that you don't distort the teapot's body shape.

1 Roll a ball of conditioned purple clay about the size of a marble between your hands until smooth and even. This ball will form the body of the teapot, which is why its shape is so important.

2 Make the base for the teapot by rolling a smaller purple ball and flattening it to about 2 mm (¹⁄₁₆ in) thick. Place the body on the base and gently press down to secure.

Attach the top first, then form your handle shape.

The pinched wide end will be fixed to the teapot's body.

3 Make the handle by rolling a string of purple clay, about 1 mm (¹⁄₃₂ in) wide and 15 mm (⅝ in) long. Flatten both ends slightly so the handle will sit neatly against the body. Attach the top of the handle at one side of the body and press down. Shape the handle and, when in position, press the opposite end in place directly underneath.

4 To shape the spout, roll a ball of purple clay and pull one end into a point to form a teardrop shape about 5 mm (³⁄₁₆ in) long and 3 mm (⅛ in) wide. Pinch the wider end of the teardrop between your fingers.

Time for tea
Silver teapots and spoons make great accompaniments to your polymer clay charms. Add in a few coloured pearls and pastel felt balls to complete the vintage look.

Handle the teapot with care to ensure it keeps its shape.

5 Use a pin to make a small hole at the pointed end of the spout. Do not pierce all the way through the spout; instead, make an indent to show where the tea would pour out.

6 Gently attach the spout to the side of the teapot opposite the handle. Handle the teapot gently so as not to distort its shape, and make sure that the spout is positioned with the pinched end at the bottom.

7 Make three leaf shapes (see page 133) from green clay and use a cocktail stick to position these on top of the teapot, using a small amount of liquid clay to secure.

Use the cocktail stick to gently nudge the flower pieces into position.

Tea rose
As an alternative flower decoration, make miniature roses by spiralling a small rose petal (see Step 3, page 44) for each bloom.

8 Insert an eyepin into the top of the teapot. Now make the flower for the top by rolling five small pale purple balls and one pink one. Place these on top of the leaves, with the pink ball in the centre of the flower.

9 Shape a small pink heart and place it in the middle of the teapot, then use the pin to texture the body of the pot. Bake the charm, following the clay manufacturer's instructions.

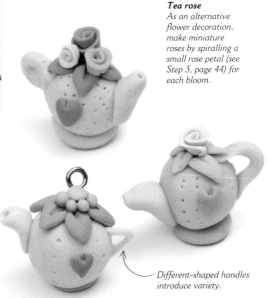

Different-shaped handles introduce variety.

Tools & materials

- Pink translucent clay
- Pink clay

- ☑ Rolling pin
- ☑ Blade
- ☑ Cocktail stick
- ☑ Eyepin

Summer shoe

This strappy little shoe is made using coloured translucent clay to give a summery feel. Once you have mastered the technique for this classic flat, try making other styles and adding high heels.

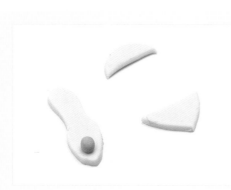

1 Use a rolling pin to roll conditioned pink translucent clay to about 1 mm (¹⁄₃₂ in) thick. Use a blade to cut out the curved shape of the shoe base, roughly 2.5 cm (1 in) long and 5 mm (³⁄₁₆ in) wide. Cut a curved shape for the toe and a slightly smaller, but similar shape for the heel. Roll a small ball of pink clay and position this at the toe end of the shoe base to help the shoe keep its shape.

2 Use a cocktail stick to help place the toe piece in position over the pink ball, ensuring that the curved edge meets the shoe base all the way around.

3 Place the heel shape in position, this time ensuring that the straight edge meets the shoe base all the way around.

Partially mix brown and yellow clays until they form a marble pattern (see page 128), for a woodgrain effect.

Skill level: ●●●

Actual size & dimensions

A Height 10 mm (³/₈ in)
B Width 25 mm (1 in)
C Depth 5 mm (³/₁₆ in)

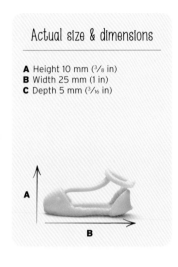

Summer sandals
Strappy summer shoes are nestled between heart and star charms and felt balls in harmonious colours on this fun, busy bracelet.

4 Cut some thin strips from the offcuts of pink translucent clay, about 2 mm (¹/₁₆ in) wide. Carefully position one strip on the shoe base close to the heel piece. Place a second strip under the toe piece.

5 Make a circle from a third thin strip and use this to join the previous strips together and form the ankle piece.

6 Use the cocktail stick to insert an eyepin carefully into the shoe base through the heel so that it doesn't poke out. Bake the charm, following the clay manufacturer's instructions.

Ballet shoes
Use pink clay to shape these gorgeous little ballet shoes, and add thin strips of clay for the ribbons.

Tools & materials

- White clay
- Mauve clay
- Tan clay
- Black clay

- ☑ Blade
- ☑ Rolling pin
- ☑ Cocktail stick
- ☑ Eyepin
- ☑ Black permanent marker

Retro alarm clock

Ring a ding ding! Time to wake up! This little alarm clock is the perfect charm for that person who is always late! Or, add it to a bracelet with an Alice in Wonderland theme, accompanied by a teapot (see pages 76–77) and cupcakes (see pages 18–19).

White clay can quickly discolour, so bake it before you continue to help keep the colour clean.

1 Roll a ball of conditioned white clay about the size of a marble between your hands. Bake the ball, following the clay manufacturer's instructions. Baking the clay now ensures that the face of the clock stays perfectly white and circular. When cool, use a blade to carefully slice down the centre of the sphere.

2 Use a rolling pin to roll out a thin layer of mauve clay, about 1 mm (¹⁄₃₂ in) thick. Use the blade to cut off a thin strip, about 3 mm (¹⁄₈ in) wide and 4 cm (1¹⁄₂ in) long. Wrap the strip around the outside edge of the clock face, pressing it on gently.

3 When the face is completely wrapped, cut the excess clay off so that the two ends meet. The join will be covered later by the alarm bells. Use a cocktail stick to help insert an eyepin slightly to one side of the join.

TIP

White clay tends to pick up dirt, so make sure your hands are extra clean. Try to use white clay before any other colour, to avoid discolouring it. Baking the clay in stages will also ensure that the white stays clean.

Actual size & dimensions

A Height 10 mm (³/₈ in)
B Width 12 mm (¹⁵/₃₂ in)
C Depth 5 mm (³/₁₆ in)

I'm late!
Place these little alarm clocks alongside slices of cake and teapots to create an Alice in Wonderland bracelet. Add a white rabbit, key and mushroom to finish the bracelet off.

Cover the join line on top of the mauve clay with one of the alarm bells.

4 For the clock's feet, roll two very small disks of tan clay, roughly 2 mm (¹/₁₆ in) wide and 1 mm (¹/₃₂ in) deep. Use the cocktail stick to position these on the bottom of the clock, opposite the eyepin.

5 Roll two slightly larger disks of tan clay, this time roughly 3 mm (¹/₈ in) wide and 2 mm (¹/₁₆ in) deep. These are the alarm bells. Place one over the join in the mauve clay and the second on the other side of the eyepin.

6 Add two tiny black clay dots, about 1 mm (¹/₃₂ in) wide, to the top of the alarm bells. Bake the complete charm and let cool. Use black permanent marker to draw on the hands, starting with a dot in the centre.

You might choose to use black clay to mould tiny clock hands.

Diamantés replace the numbers here.

What time is it?
You could choose to draw a time on the clock face that has a particular meaning, perhaps the time you met for your first date, or the time a child was born.

Cute camera

This snappy little camera is a flashy addition to your charm collection. Although making it involves some complex steps, the finished camera looks so good you'll want to use it!

Tools & materials

- Green clay
- Grey clay
- Black clay
- Translucent liquid clay

- ☑ Rolling pin
- ☑ Blade
- ☑ Cocktail stick
- ☑ Eyepin
- ☑ Black permanent marker

Actual size & dimensions

A Height 10 mm (³/₈ in)
B Width 15 mm (⁵/₈ in)
C Depth 5 mm (³/₁₆ in)

1 Use a rolling pin to roll out conditioned green clay to about 3 mm (¹/₈ in) thick and 2 cm (³/₄ in) square. Use a blade to cut a rectangle 1.5 cm x 8 mm (⁵/₈ x ⁵/₁₆ in) for the camera body. Cut a 3 mm (¹/₈ in) square from the leftover clay for the viewfinder.

2 Use the blade to cut a slot out of the centre top of the camera, 1 mm (¹/₃₂ in) deep and 2 mm (¹/₁₆ in) wide. Remove the excess clay and pop the viewfinder clay square into the slot.

3 Use the rolling pin to roll conditioned grey clay out to about the thickness of a playing card. Cut out a thin strip of grey clay, 2 mm (¹/₁₆ in) wide and 2 cm (³/₄ in) long. Wrap this around the top of the camera.

4 Roll a ball of green clay about 3 mm (¹/₈ in) wide and flatten it slightly with your finger. Place this centrally under the viewfinder and press gently down to secure it.

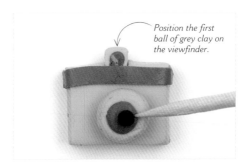

Position the first ball of grey clay on the viewfinder.

5 Roll a small ball of grey clay about 1 mm (¹/₃₂ in) wide and use a cocktail stick to help press it onto the viewfinder. Roll a second, slightly larger, grey ball, 2 mm (¹/₁₆ in) wide, and press it onto the end of the lens. Finally, roll a small ball of black clay the same size as the first grey ball and press this into the middle of the lens.

6 Insert an eyepin into the viewfinder from the top. Do this slowly so that you do not distort the camera's finished shape.

Make sure the translucent clay stays on the lens area.

7 Use the cocktail stick to apply translucent liquid clay to the end of the lens, which, when baked, will give the lens a shiny, glasslike appearance.

8 Use the blade to carefully cut the grey strip around the viewfinder, and to trim the top of the green clay in line with the grey strip. Bake the charm, following the manufacturer's instructions. Once cool, use black permanent marker to add the finishing details.

Happy snappy
If you find slotting in the viewfinder too tricky, keep the camera as a rectangle and add the viewfinder to the main body of the camera. Made in different colours, these charms make the perfect gift for the photography lover you know!

Tools & materials

- ● Brown clay
- ● Mauve clay

- ☑ Blade
- ☑ Eyepin
- ☑ Cocktail stick
- ☑ Pencil sharpener

School pencil

If you love to draw, these cute little pencils could be just the thing for you. They also make a perfect gift for the arty person in your life, or you could make them as a present for your favourite teacher! Team them with an apple and a gold star for the perfect 'thank you' gift.

Only slice halfway through the depth.

1 Roll conditioned brown clay into a log about 2 cm (³⁄₄ in) long and 5 mm (³⁄₁₆ in) wide. This will form the wooden part of the pencil.

2 Use a blade to cut down the length of the pencil, but only cut halfway through the depth. Carefully open the slit. If the clay is not soft enough where you open it, it may break and crumble. If this happens, start again, but roll the clay between your hands a little first.

3 Roll a snake of conditioned mauve clay a little longer than the brown log but only about 2 mm (¹⁄₁₆ in) wide. Place the mauve shape inside the brown shape.

Position thin strips of coloured clay next to each other all around the finished pencil before baking.

Stationery style
It is easy to play with the basic techniques of this project to make different styles of pencil, or to add a pen to your stationery collection.

Press a thin log together with a slightly wider one to form a pen shape.

Skill level: ● ● ●

Actual size & dimensions

A Height 6 mm (¼ in)
B Width 25 mm (1 in)
C Depth 6 mm (¼ in)

Pencil chain
Place these tiny pencils on a necklace chain, perfect for your inner artist. Add more and more pencils whenever you want to.

Don't worry about the ends yet.

Sharpen the end of the cool charm to reveal the lead and finish the pencil.

4 Close the brown clay around the mauve clay so that no mauve can be seen. Gently roll the shape back and forth on a hard surface to make it smooth and rounded again. Don't roll too much, since you do not want it to get longer, just smoother.

5 Neaten the ends by trimming each one with the blade. Insert an eyepin into one end of the pencil and bake the charm, following the clay manufacturer's instructions. Once the pencil has cooled, sharpen it as you would a normal pencil.

6 As a variation, once the pencil has been baked and sharpened, cover it with a layer of clay in the same colour as the pencil lead. Roll a thin sheet in this colour and use a zigzag blade to trim away a line from the top. Then wrap the sheet around the pencil and bake again for ten minutes.

Airmail envelope

One of the best things about this charm is that it can be personalized with the recipient's name and where they live. Or use a nickname and the name of their favourite city or holiday destination.

Tools & materials

- ● Beige clay
- ● Red clay
- ○ White clay
- ● Blue clay

- ☑ Rolling pin
- ☑ Blade
- ☑ Cocktail stick
- ☑ Eyepin
- ☑ Black permanent marker

Actual size & dimensions

A Height 15 mm (⅝ in)
B Width 15 mm (⅝ in)
C Depth 3 mm (⅛ in)

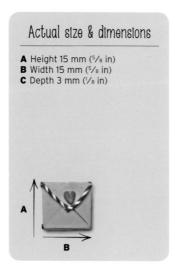

1 Use a rolling pin to roll conditioned beige clay as thinly as possible, roughly 1 mm (¹⁄₃₂ in). Use a blade to cut the thin clay into a 3 cm (1¼ in) square.

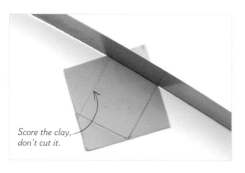

Score the clay, don't cut it.

2 Use the blade very gently to score a line diagonally across each corner of the square, making the clay easier to fold.

3 Fold along the score lines one at a time to create the envelope shape.

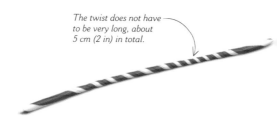

The twist does not have to be very long, about 5 cm (2 in) in total.

4 Roll three thin strings, about 1 mm (¹⁄₃₂ in) thick, of conditioned red, white and blue clay. Gently twist them together between your fingers, rolling each end in a different direction to the other.

Skill level: ● ● ●

Absence makes the heart grow fonder
Heart charms, bluebirds and envelopes combine to create a romantic, travel-themed bracelet.

5 Lay the clay twist across the top edge of the front of the envelope, cut it to size and press in place. Repeat for the bottom edge.

6 Mould a small amount of red clay into a heart shape, about 3 mm (⅛ in) long, and use a cocktail stick to position this where a postage stamp would usually go.

Sent with love
Develop the postage theme with a parcel or stamp charm. A heart motif, painted on using liquid clay mixed with pink clay, clearly shows the thought behind the gift.

7 Use the remaining red-white-and-blue twist to line the fold edges on the back of the envelope, and add another small heart. Use the cocktail stick to guide an eyepin into place through the top edge of the envelope. Alternatively, use the cocktail stick to make a hole in the top of the envelope.

8 Follow the clay manufacturer's instructions to bake the charm. Once cooled, use black permanent marker to add in a name and address.

Wrap a pre-baked clay box shape with a thin layer of caramel clay.

Tools & materials

- Beige clay
- Pastel pink clay

- ☑ Rolling pin
- ☑ 1 cm (³⁄₈ in) round cutter
- ☑ Extruder with 1 mm (¹⁄₃₂ in) plate
- ☑ Cocktail stick
- ☑ Eyepin

Cotton reel

The culture of 'make do and mend' has not only gained in popularity in recent times, but has even become fashionable, which means more and more people are becoming passionate about sewing, knitting and crochet. Sewing accessories make great charms, as this cotton reel demonstrates.

1 Use a rolling pin to roll conditioned beige clay to a thickness of about 2 mm (¹⁄₁₆ in). Use a 1 cm (³⁄₈ in) round cutter to cut two circles out of the rolled clay. Use your hands to roll a ball of beige clay slightly smaller than a marble, then shape this into a log, about 1 cm (³⁄₈ in) tall and 8 mm (⁵⁄₁₆ in) wide.

2 Centre the log on one of the beige circles, then place the other circle centrally on top of the log.

3 Roll well-conditioned pastel pink clay into a marble-sized ball and place this inside an extruder fitted with a 1 mm (¹⁄₃₂ in) plate. Turn the handle until all of the clay has been extruded.

Skill level: ● ● ●

Actual size & dimensions

A Height 15 mm (⁵/₈ in)
B Width 10 mm (³/₈ in)
C Depth 10 mm (³/₈ in)

Sewing bee
This haberdashery-themed bracelet is full of relevant charms. Place buttons and silver charms among your polymer clay charms to make interesting combinations.

Carefully align each wrap on top of the one before.

4 Starting at the base, wrap the pink extruded clay carefully around the beige cylinder, lining it up neatly so the clay wraps sit snugly on top of each other. Wrap fairly tightly, so that the clay does not look baggy.

5 Once you have wrapped neatly to the top of the reel, add a few more wraps over the previous ones to add width and give the charm a realistic look.

6 Use a cocktail stick to guide an eyepin into the top centre of the charm. Bake the clay, following the manufacturer's instructions.

To make a ball of yarn, wrap your strands of clay around a clay ball.

Cotton colours
You can make cotton reels in various colours, or use extruder plates of different sizes to create thicker yarns. Make a basket to put them in, following the instructions for the bird's nest on pages 48–49, but pile on a few extra wraps.

Knitted heart

Knitted-effect texture looks fabulous, and in clay form you might be fooled into thinking it is difficult to achieve. These sweet little knitted hearts are made using an extruder and a simple twisting technique.

Tools & materials

● Pink clay
● Purple clay

☑ Extruder with 1 mm (¹⁄₃₂ in) multiple string plate
☑ Blade
☑ Rolling pin
☑ Heart-shaped cutter
☑ Cocktail stick
☑ Eyepin

Actual size & dimensions

A Height 17 mm (¹¹⁄₁₆ in)
B Width 15 mm (⁵⁄₈ in)
C Depth 3 mm (¹⁄₈ in)

1 Take a piece of pink and a piece of purple clay, each about the size of a marble. Condition each piece in your hands until really soft and pliable. Once the clay is warm, place both pieces inside an extruder and turn the handle until all the clay is pushed out.

One finger rolls up while the other rolls down.

2 Take two strands of clay and gently twist them together between your fingers, rolling each hand in a different direction to the other. Take note of which hand rolls upward and which hand rolls downward. Twist half of your strands in this direction and put them in a pile.

Keep your twists in separate piles determined by the direction they were rolled.

3 Twist together pairs of the remaining strands, this time twisting in the opposite direction, so the hand that rolled upward last time will now roll downward, and vice versa. Put these twists in a separate pile.

4 Use a blade to cut the twisted strands into sections 2 cm (³⁄₄ in) long. Make sure you keep your piles separate.

Use different cutters to create assorted knitted items.

Alternating the strands based on the twist direction gives the knitted effect.

Make sure the knitting is straight inside the cutter.

TIP

Using the extruder is an easy and quick way of making lots of thin strands of clay that are all the same size. If you do not have an extruder, this charm is still easy to produce, you just need to spend a little bit of extra time making thin clay strands by hand. For a similar two-colour effect, twist together different-coloured strands.

5 Use a rolling pin to roll a thin sheet of conditioned pink clay, about 1 mm ($^1/_{32}$ in) thick and 2 cm ($^3/_4$ in) square. Use a cocktail stick to place a strand from one pile next to a strand from the other pile on top of the pink base. Make sure the stands touch. Continue alternating the strands to cover the base.

6 Once the entire base is covered with twisted stands, gently press over the top of the base to ensure that it is fixed down well. Position a heart-shaped cutter over the clay and check that the knitting is running straight to your cutter and not at an angle.

7 Press the cutter gently through all the layers, then remove the cutter. If the shape gets stuck in the cutter, turn it over and use a piece of spare clay to gently and evenly push the shape out.

8 Using the cocktail stick, insert an eyepin into the top of the heart. Bake the charm, following the clay manufacturer's instructions.

Wear it with pride
Simply glue your knitted heart onto a flat-pad finding to create this wonderful ring. Knitwear is gaining in popularity, and what better way to support the movement than by wearing it?

Russian doll

These lovable charms can be made in sets from large to small, just like the stacking dolls they are based on, and are relatively easy to make with only a few simple steps! Why not make a family of dolls and hang them from a bracelet or brooch pin, or even team them with a folk-style bird charm (see pages 60-61) to make a tradition-inspired design.

- Pale green clay
- Flesh-coloured clay
- Dark brown clay
- Red clay
- Mauve clay
- Green clay
- Translucent liquid clay

☑ Cocktail stick
☑ Eyepin

Actual size & dimensions

A Height 20 mm (³/₄ in)
B Width 10 mm (³/₈ in)
C Depth 10 mm (³/₈ in)

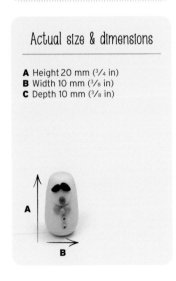

Flatten the ball with your finger, aiming to make a round shape.

1 For the body of the doll, form conditioned pale green clay into an egg shape about 12.5 mm (½ in) long and 10 mm (³/₈ in) wide.

2 For the doll's face, roll a flesh-coloured clay sphere about the size of a pea, then use the flat of your finger to squash the ball until it is 1 mm (¹/₃₂ in) thick.

3 Form the hair by making two dark brown teardrop shapes, each about 3 mm (¹/₈ in) long. Use a cocktail stick and a little translucent liquid clay to gently press the hair shapes in place at the top of the face.

4 Roll a small red dot and position it on the face where the mouth should be. Press gently down into the middle of the dot with the cocktail stick to secure it and form the lips.

Keep the shape of the face round by handling it as little as possible.

Cute and simple
Add intrigue to a charm bracelet by threading coloured cord through the links of the chain. Felt balls fill the gaps in this charm bracelet to keep the look simple and clean.

5 Carefully pick up the face and place it on the narrowest end of the pale green egg shape. Press down gently. Try to keep the face as round and undistorted as possible by handling it as few times as you can.

6 Make a little bow tie for your charm by rolling mauve clay into two tiny teardrop shapes and one small dot. Place the two teardrops under the chin of the doll with the dot in between. Secure with a small amount of translucent liquid clay.

TIP
A more ornate Russian doll can be created by applying acrylic paint to the baked charm, introducing a more intricate and unusual design.

Doll decorations
Using just the basic shapes of teardrops, circles and balls, a host of different decorations can be made for your Russian dolls.

7 For the little buttons, roll two small balls of green clay and place them on the doll in line with the dot in the middle of the bow.

8 Press the cocktail stick into the centre of each button, as you did with the mouth. Insert an eyepin into the top of the Russian doll in line with the face, so that the charm will hang straight. Bake the charm following the clay manufacturer's instructions.

Use tiny balls for hair.

An arrangement of balls of clay can make a flower instead of a bow tie.

Faceted bead

With just a few steps and very simple techniques, you cannot go wrong when making these angular charms. The modern little shapes fit right in with current trends, and can be grouped together in any number of colour combinations. For some great results, try not to overthink the design of this bead, but let the blade lead you.

1 When making this geometric bead, try to handle the conditioned clay as little as possible so that it remains quite firm and not too soft, otherwise you will not be able to create the necessary straight, angular edges. Start by rolling a ball of magenta clay about the size of a marble.

2 Place the ball on the work surface and use a blade to cut off the first curved side.

3 Always cut straight down and from the same position. Make sure you press the blade down firmly all the way through the clay in one smooth cut. Continue to cut off all of the curved sides.

TIP

If the clay becomes too soft, place it on a piece of paper to absorb some of the moisture, then leave to firm up in the refrigerator for about 30 minutes.

It is fine to slice some beads more than others.

Vary the angles you cut at and the amount you slice off.

Never-ending creations
With this simple sculpting technique, no two beads are ever exactly the same. The wealth and variety of shapes that can be created is almost infinite.

Skill level: ● ● ●

Actual size & dimensions

A Height 12.5 mm (½ in)
B Width 12.5 mm (½ in)
C Depth 10 mm (³⁄₈ in)

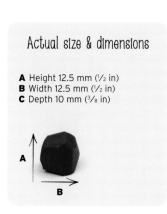

Mix it up
These beads work well together mixed in any number of colourways. Here a contemporary palette combines pastel and striking hues to great effect.

4 Place the bead on one of the newly straight sides and repeat the cutting process. Each time the clay is turned it should by sliced no less than four times, otherwise it will risk looking like a cube.

5 Continue cutting and rotating until there are no curved sides remaining.

6 Use a cocktail stick to help insert an eyepin into one side of the bead. Bake the clay, following the manufacturer's instructions.

TIP

To hang the bead horizontally, insert the eyepin all the way through the clay and remove it before baking. You will then be able to thread the bead, as an alternative to using it as a charm.

Charming button

These fun little shapes can actually be used as buttons, not just as charms! A word of warning, though: remember to hand wash the items in warm water, since a washing machine may damage the buttons.

Tools & materials

- ● Pink clay
- ○ Pastel pink clay
- ● Purple clay
- ○ Green clay

- ☑ Rolling pin
- ☑ Cocktail stick
- ☑ 1.5 cm (⅝ in) shaped cutter

Actual size & dimensions

A Height 15 mm (⅝ in)
B Width 15 mm (⅝ in)
C Depth 15 mm (⅝ in)

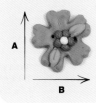

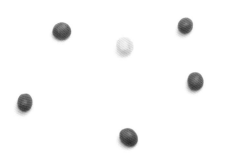

1 Prepare the elements that make up the button's flower decoration by rolling tiny balls of conditioned clay, about 2 mm (¹⁄₁₆ in) wide - five in pink and one in pastel pink.

2 Use a rolling pin to roll out purple clay for the base of the button, to a thickness of about 2 mm (¹⁄₁₆ in). Use a cocktail stick to position the pastel pink ball on the purple clay, with the five bright pink balls around it.

3 Make two green leaves (see page 133). Place one leaf at the side of the flower and gently press it down with the cocktail stick until attached.

Think about how you position the second leaf in relation to the shape you will be cutting out.

4 Position the second leaf on the opposite side of the flower, bearing in mind the shape and size of your cutter: make sure it can fit over the flower and leaves motif without cutting through the design.

Skill level: ●●●

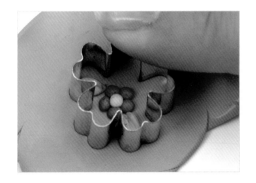

Full of fun
Pastel-coloured buttons in a variety of shapes and sizes combine to make a wonderfully full bracelet.

Instead of using an eyepin, you can insert a jump ring through the button's hole.

5 Hover the cutter over the flower, looking down into it to correct any positioning issues before pressing down. When you are happy with the positioning, press down through the clay until the cutter hits the work surface.

6 Pull the cutter straight out of the clay and the shape should remain on the work surface. If it does not, turn the cutter upside down and gently press at the edges on the wrong side of the shape until it drops out.

TIP
You can use a cocktail stick or other tools to texture buttons before baking. Or, try baking plain buttons and using acrylic paint to decorate them.

Push the cocktail stick all the way through the clay.

7 Use the cocktail stick to make a hole on each side of the flower. If you want your button to be a charm, insert an eyepin now. Bake the clay, following the manufacturer's instructions.

Insert an eyepin before you bake the clay if you want to use your button as a charm.

Decorate your buttons using single flowers or a few.

Cute as a button
If you need an excuse to build on your stock of cutters, this is it. You can make buttons using any of the great cutter shapes that are available.

Tools & materials

- White clay

- ☑ Rolling pin
- ☑ 1.5 cm (⅝ in) flower cutter
- ☑ Cocktail stick
- ☑ Paintbrush
- ☑ Pink, lilac and purple alcohol inks
- ☑ Varnish

Colourwash flower

This charm is all about the decoration. The shape is a simple cut-out flower, but the charm comes to life with the addition of alcohol inks that flow into each other and create a colourwash effect, similar to that seen in a watercolour painting. This simple but effective embellishing method can easily be transferred to other charm projects.

Don't paint the ink on, dot it.

1 Use a rolling pin to roll conditioned white clay out to a thickness of about 2 mm (¹⁄₁₆ in), trying to keep the surface even. Gently press a 1.5 cm (⅝ in) flower cutter through the clay and remove the clay shape.

2 Pierce a hole in the top of one of the petals with a cocktail stick, then bake the bead, following the clay manufacturer's instructions.

3 Once the baked bead has cooled, use a paintbrush to dot pink alcohol ink over the surface, trying not to apply too much. You are aiming for a textured coverage, not an even spread of ink.

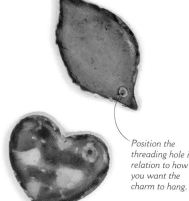

Position the threading hole in relation to how you want the charm to hang.

Versatile style
This decorating technique is effective on any number of charm shapes.

Skill level: ●●●

Actual size & dimensions

A Height 15 mm (⁵/₈ in)
B Width 15 mm (⁵/₈ in)
C Depth 2 mm (¹/₁₆ in)

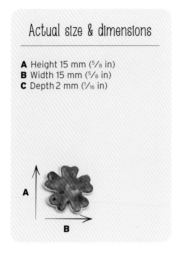

Thread a jump ring through the hole made in Step 2 to attach the charms to the jewellery.

A wash of colour
Use crystal beads to bring out the colours in your colourwash charms and liven up the bracelet.

The second ink colour spreads into the first.

4 Now use the brush to dot lilac ink onto sections of the bead. The ink will spread and have the appearance of watercolour. Work quickly, since the ink will only blend while wet; if the charm becomes too wet with ink, however, you won't get the mottled effect.

5 Move swiftly on to the next colour, dark purple, dotting this on in sections: the more the ink dries, the less it will spread.

6 When you are happy with your ink effect, leave to dry, then coat the surface of the charm with varnish.

The watercolour effect
The alcohol inks have a mind of their own, so don't expect the same result twice. Using this simple technique, and the same inks, you can create charms that complement each other but are unique at the same time.

Choose your palette
Experiment with other mixes of ink colours to see what can be achieved.

Textured bead

A basic ball-shaped bead provides the perfect surface for decorating with texturing techniques. This bead features a structured, ordered pattern of decoration, but you might prefer to throw caution to the wind with a random approach.

Tools & materials

● Pink clay

☑ Cocktail stick

Actual size & dimensions

A Height 15 mm (⁵⁄₈ in)
B Width 15 mm (⁵⁄₈ in)
C Depth 15 mm (⁵⁄₈ in)

1 Roll a ball of conditioned pink clay between your hands to about marble size. Apply gentle pressure to the ball to ensure that it keeps its shape, while also smoothing any cracks.

2 Roll 20 small balls of pink clay, roughly 2 mm (¹⁄₁₆ in) round. Visualize the marble-sized ball in quarters, and, in the next steps, aim to fill each quarter with decoration, to ensure that the bead is evenly covered.

3 Working on the first quarter, place five of the small balls in a line on the larger ball of clay. Press them down gently so that they don't fall off at this stage.

4 Gently press a cocktail stick into the centre of each of the small balls to shape them and fix them firmly in place.

Skill level: ●●●

Simple but effective
Different textured beads look great when mixed together on a charm bracelet. To use them as charms, add an eyepin after baking (see page 123), with a little bead added to the loop.

5 Roll even smaller pink balls and place these between the balls applied in the previous steps. Use the cocktail stick to help position the balls, then press down gently with a finger.

Take care to keep the line of dots straight.

6 Now use the cocktail stick to dimple the surface of the bead in a line next to the applied smaller balls.

7 Repeat Steps 3–6 to fill the remaining three-quarters of the bead with raised decoration and texturing.

Twist the cocktail stick as you slowly and carefully push it all the way through.

8 Use the cocktail stick to make a hole all the way through the clay bead, gently pushing and twisting the stick as you go. Bake the bead, following the manufacturer's instructions.

Twist thin slices of clay and curl them on the surface of the bead.

Press a ball tool into a tiny circle of clay to create a petal shape. Combine five petals on the bead for each flower.

Indent the surface of a ball of clay with star shapes.

Adding and taking away
As the project illustrates, simple clay beads can be textured with additions and indentations. Here are some other ideas.

Circus tent

What could be cuter than a vintage-style circus tent with a flag to match? Accompany this perfect big top with circus animals, or make a bracelet from a row of different-coloured tents. Bear in mind that the modelling and shaping techniques used to make this charm can be a little tricky to master, so try not to get disheartened.

Tools & materials

● Red clay
○ White clay
● Blue clay

☑ Rolling pin
☑ 1.5 cm (⅝ in) round cutter
☑ Blade
☑ Cocktail stick
☑ Eyepin

Actual size & dimensions

A Height 25 mm (1 in)
B Width 15 mm (⅝ in)
C Depth 15 mm (⅝ in)

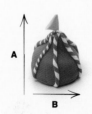

1 Use a rolling pin to roll out conditioned red clay until it is 5 mm (³⁄₁₆ in) thick and at least 2 cm (¾ in) wide. Use a 1.5 cm (⅝ in) round cutter to cut out a disk of clay to form the base of the tent.

Flatten the edges of the ball only, then pull up the centre.

2 Roll a marble-sized ball of red clay, flatten it around the edges, then pull it into a point at the top. This will form the roof of the tent.

3 Centre the round cutter over the point of the roof and push down to trim away the excess clay.

Use your fingers to smooth over the join.

4 Place the roof on top of the base and press together gently. Use your fingers to press the sides together until smooth and rounded and the join is no longer visible.

Placing charms on an eyepin between two chains means the necklace will hang evenly.

Showtime
Surround your circus tent with little silver carousels and stars to complete the showtime feel.

Keep twisting until you are happy with the striped effect.

Before pressing the strips into position, check that they are equally spaced apart around the tent, and adjust with the cocktail stick if necessary.

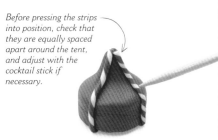

5 Roll a string of conditioned white clay that is 5 cm (2 in) long and 1 mm (1/32 in) wide. Repeat with red clay. Place the two strings next to each other and twist them together until striped and well combined.

6 Use a blade to cut six strips of the striped string to fit the height of the tent. Position the strips equally spaced around the tent, using a cocktail stick to make adjustments.

Tent extensions
It is easy to adapt the circus tent to your own designs. A teepee makes a fun tent variation, decorated after baking with felt-tip pens.

7 Roll out blue clay to a thickness of 1 mm (1/32 in). Use the blade to cut out two triangles, with each side about 3 mm (1/8 in) long. Sandwich the triangles around an eyepin, just below the loop, to form the flag.

8 Using the cocktail stick to enable careful placement, insert the eyepin into the top of the tent. Bake the charm, following the clay manufacturer's instructions.

Stripes of clay replace the twists, and there's a few more of them!

Celebration bunting

Bunting makes everything better, and these quick and easy charms can be made in any colour for any occasion. The bunting looks great on its own charm bracelet, or can be nestled in between other charms.

Tools & materials

- Vibrant green clay
- Purple clay
- Pink clay
- Blue clay

- ☑ Rolling pin
- ☑ Blade
- ☑ Cocktail stick

Actual size & dimensions

A Height 20 mm (³/₄ in)
B Width 15 mm (⁵/₈ in)
C Depth 2 mm (¹/₁₆ in)

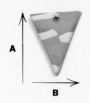

1 Use a rolling pin to roll conditioned vibrant green clay into a slab about 2 mm (¹/₁₆ in) deep, 1 cm (³/₈ in) wide and 2 cm (³/₄ in) long. Set aside and repeat to make slabs of purple, pink and blue clay.

2 Press the clay slabs together, trying to keep the ends and sides lined up. Press gently on all sides to help the clay stick together.

This will form the pattern for the bunting.

3 Position the stack upright on the work surface and use a blade to cut it in half. Place one half on top of the other and press down. Squeeze the clay between your fingers until it is about the same size and shape that it was originally.

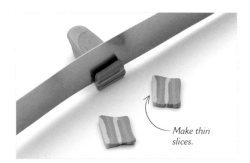

Make thin slices.

4 Use the blade to cut thin slices of the layered clay, aiming to cut as thinly as possible to give you plenty of slices.

Skill level: ●●●

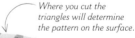

Place jump rings through the links in the necklace so that the charms stay where they are supposed to.

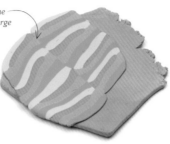

Roll over the slices to merge the joins.

Celebrate in style
Thread jump rings through the hole made in Step 8 to attach your bunting charms to a necklace, accompanied by felt balls that bring out the clay colours.

5 Use the rolling pin to roll purple clay to a thickness of about 2 mm (¹/₁₆ in), and place the striped slices on the purple clay as close together as possible, so that the base does not show through. A 4 cm (1½ in) square of purple clay will house four striped slices and make three bunting triangles.

6 Gently roll the rolling pin over the clay. This will make the joins in the clay merge together so that there are no gaps. The more gently you press, the less the shape will distort.

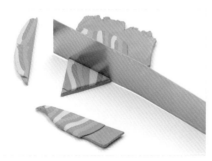

Where you cut the triangles will determine the pattern on the surface.

7 Use the blade to cut triangles from the striped clay, trying to make sure that the sides and angles are even. If preferred, make a template from card and cut around that to ensure all the triangles are equal.

8 Use a cocktail stick to make a hole at the top-centre of each bunting triangle to ensure that the charm will hang straight. Bake the clay, following the manufacturer's instructions.

Changing track
Cut the triangles with the stripes going in different directions for a little variation.

Patterned Easter egg

This pastel patterned egg charm looks great at any time of year, but also makes a fun Easter gift, without the added calories! The patterning looks challenging to achieve, but is easier than you might think, but we won't tell anyone!

Tools & materials

- White clay
- Pastel blue clay
- Pastel yellow clay
- Pastel pink clay
- Spare clay

☑ Blade
☑ Extruder with square plate
☑ Cocktail stick
☑ Eyepin

Actual size & dimensions

A Height 20 mm (³⁄₄ in)
B Width 15 mm (⁵⁄₈ in)
C Depth 15 mm (⁵⁄₈ in)

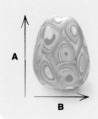

The pieces should be of a width that will fit easily into the extruder.

1 Condition a piece of white clay about the size of two marbles between your hands until soft. Repeat with the pastel blue, pastel yellow and pastel pink clays. Shape the clay pieces a little further until they are about 1 cm (³⁄₈ in) wide – a good size for fitting into an extruder.

2 Use a blade to cut the clay shapes into slices, about 5 mm (³⁄₁₆ in) thick.

3 Arrange the slices in a long line in your preferred colour order.

4 Fit the extruder with a square plate, then place the line of coloured clays inside. Keep twisting the handle until all of the clay has been extruded.

Skill level: ● ● ●

Spring theme
Pastel colours are the perfect choice for Easter-themed charms, since they are symbolic of new growth. Team the eggs with little rabbit charms to complete the look.

On extrusion, the clays have merged into some great patterns.

5 Now cut the extruded cane into four equal lengths. Place these lengths next to each other and gently press them together until each one is attached to its neighbour.

Apply gentle pressure to all four sides until the canes resemble one complete block.

6 Cut this grouping of canes in half lengthways and stack one half on top of the other. Gently press down on all sides so that the two halves become one.

7 Now use the blade to cut slices of this cane as thinly as possible. Roll a ball of spare clay to the size of a marble and wrap the thin slices around the outside until the surface is completely covered.

Keep gently rolling until you can no longer see any join lines.

8 Roll the covered ball between your hands to merge the edges of the slices and give a smooth, seamless covering. Press very gently so as not to distort the pattern or shape.

9 Pinch the top of the ball between your fingers to draw it into an egg shape. Use a cocktail stick to help insert an eyepin through the egg from the top, then bake the clay, following the manufacturer's instructions.

Bright and bold
Bright colours and bold patterns also look great on egg shapes. Roll slices of the patterned clay over a ball of clay and mould the egg shape in the usual way.

Make a Skinner blend (see page 129) and shape into a cube. Stretch the cube, then make your slices.

Halloween pumpkin

Carving a jack-o'-lantern is a Halloween tradition, but this little fellow is far from scary. Your pumpkin charm can be given very different characteristics simply by changing the marks you make for its face.

Tools & materials

● Orange clay
● Green clay

☑ Blade
☑ Cocktail stick
☑ Eyepin
☑ Black permanent marker

Actual size & dimensions

A Height 12.5 mm (½ in)
B Width 15 mm (⅝ in)
C Depth 15 mm (⅝ in)

1 Soften a marble-sized piece of orange clay between your hands, then roll it into a smooth ball.

2 Use a blade to indent the clay in sections all around the ball. Press gently and do not let the blade go too far into the clay: you do not want to cut right through the ball.

The indentations open up slightly when you press down on the clay.

3 When all your indentations have been made, press down gently on the top of the charm with a finger. This will cause the sections to open slightly so your ball now looks like a pumpkin.

4 Use a cocktail stick to make a hole in the centre-top of the pumpkin that goes halfway through the charm.

Skill level: ● ● ●

Halloween theme
Orange and black are the obvious colour choices for Halloween. Team your pumpkins with felt balls and little silver witch charms to make a wonderfully spooky bracelet.

Don't worry about uniformity, just make sure all the spikes are similar in size.

Use the cocktail stick to curl the spikes a little, so that they look natural.

5 Roll five small spikes of green clay between your fingers.

6 Use the cocktail stick to position the spikes around the edge of the hole at the top of the charm. Stand one of the spikes up to act as the stalk.

Mixed motifs
These days people are getting far more artistic with their jack-o'-lantern designs. You can use your pen with a flourish, or make shapes using thinly rolled black clay.

Mould a gourd shape for more of a squash than a pumpkin.

7 Push an eyepin into the charm behind the stalk, using the cocktail stick to position it carefully. Bake the charm, following the clay manufacturer's instructions.

8 Once the baked charm has cooled, use black permanent marker to draw a scary face on the pumpkin, in true Halloween style.

Gingerbread house

A gingerbread house, covered with confectionary treats, is a Christmas delight. This polymer clay version is perhaps a little easier to construct than its edible counterpart, but looks just as sweet, and makes a great festive gift for a baking loved-one!

Tools & materials

- Brown clay
- Red clay
- White clay
- Dark brown clay

- ☑ Blade
- ☑ Cocktail stick
- ☑ Eyepin

Actual size & dimensions

A Height 12.5 mm (½ in)
B Width 10 mm (³⁄₈ in)
C Depth 12.5 mm (½ in)

1 Use a blade to cut out a cube of conditioned brown clay, just under 1 cm (³⁄₈ in) wide, tall and deep.

2 Cut off a diagonal section from each side of the cube to form the roof.

3 Roll a red and a white string of conditioned clay on the work surface, about 1 mm (¹⁄₃₂ in) thick. Place the strings next to each other then gently twist them together between your fingers, rolling each end in a different direction to the other.

Leave the bottom edge unembellished.

4 Lay the twisted string up the side of the house, cut it to size and press in place. Repeat along all the straight edges of the house, except the bottom edge.

Festive fun
Thread red ribbon through the links of a chain and centre the gingerbread house alongside little hearts and, of course, gingerbread men.

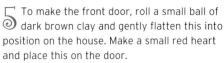

5 To make the front door, roll a small ball of dark brown clay and gently flatten this into position on the house. Make a small red heart and place this on the door.

6 Use a cocktail stick as a texturing tool, gently pressing it into the surface of the clay to dimple it, where required.

7 Add another small heart on each side of the roof and, if there is room, a few slices cut from the red-and-white twisted string.

8 Use the cocktail stick to insert an eyepin through the house at the centre of the roof's point, to ensure that the charm will hang straight. Bake the charm, following the clay manufacturer's instructions

Rainbow house
A multicoloured house is a fun alternative. Press tiny pieces of coloured clay all over the roof as tiles, and decorate the front with colourful canes.

Tools & materials

- Green clay
- Red clay
- Yellow clay
- Brown clay

- ☑ Rolling pin
- ☑ Blade
- ☑ Cocktail stick
- ☑ Eyepin

Christmas tree

This iconic symbol of Christmas spirit is made in several stages, including separate baking of parts. The different techniques make a unique and adorable little decorated tree.

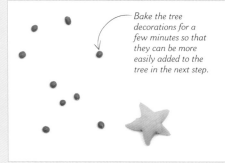

Bake the tree decorations for a few minutes so that they can be more easily added to the tree in the next step.

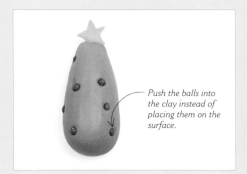

Push the balls into the clay instead of placing them on the surface.

1 Use your hands to mould a marble-sized ball of conditioned green clay into a cone shape. Roll it over the work surface until it is about 1.5 cm (⅝ in) long and narrower at one end than the other.

2 Roll tiny balls of conditioned red clay, about 1 mm (¹/₃₂ in) round: as many as you need to decorate your tree. Use a rolling pin to roll yellow clay to a thickness of 1 mm (¹/₃₂ in), and use a blade to cut out a star shape, about 3 mm (⅛ in) wide. Bake the star and the red balls for about five minutes, until hard.

3 Press the baked red balls into the green cone as the baubles for the tree. Spread them out evenly all over the tree, and press in gently until they are flush with the surface. Push the baked star into the top of the tree, pushing one spike in until secure.

Skill level: ● ● ●

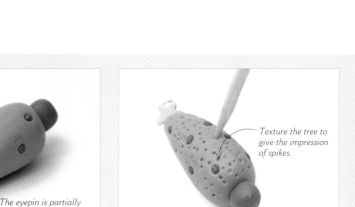

Winter wonderland
On a necklace, hang bugle beads, silver snowman charms and other decorations equally spaced on either side of your Christmas tree, to ensure that the necklace will hang evenly.

Actual size & dimensions

A Height 25 mm (1 in)
B Width 10 mm (³/₈ in)
C Depth 10 mm (³/₈ in)

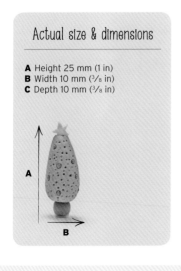

The eyepin is partially hidden by the star.

Texture the tree to give the impression of spikes.

4 Roll a ball of conditioned brown clay, about 5 mm (³/₁₆ in) round, and press this onto the bottom of the tree for the trunk.

5 Use a cocktail stick to insert an eyepin into the top of the tree behind the star, which will hide most of the finding.

6 Press gently into the surface of the tree with the cocktail stick to texture it and give it the spiked look that is characteristic of Christmas trees. Bake the whole charm, following the clay manufacturer's instructions.

Stick diamantés around the tree like sparkly tinsel.

Candy canes and a gold star: a classic.

Trio of trees
Everyone decorates their Christmas tree in their own style, and the same can be true with these miniature versions. Use glue to stick on pre-baked decorations.

Christmas stocking

Everyone likes a little sparkle at Christmas, so this stocking is made using a glittery clay in a festive red. The little white balls along the cuff add some depth to this predominantly flat motif, while also suggesting a fluffy, furry finishing touch.

Actual size & dimensions

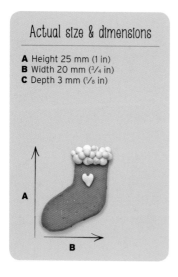

A Height 25 mm (1 in)
B Width 20 mm (¾ in)
C Depth 3 mm (⅛ in)

1 Use a rolling pin to roll conditioned red glitter clay out to a thickness of about 2 mm (¹⁄₁₆ in).

2 Draw your stocking shape on some card, about 2.5 cm (1 in) in height and 2 cm (¾ in) at the widest point. Cut this out as a template. Place the template on the red clay sheet and use a blade to cut around it.

3 Use a finger to smooth out the edges of the cut shape, ensuring there are no jagged areas.

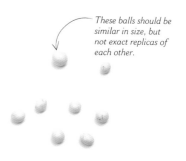

These balls should be similar in size, but not exact replicas of each other.

4 Roll about ten small balls of conditioned white clay. They do not need to be exactly the same size, but should be in the region of 3 mm (⅛ in) round.

Skill level: ● ● ●

Festive fancy
Sticking with a simple palette of red, white and silver, this charm combines beautifully with snowflakes, candy canes and fluffy felt balls.

5 Position the balls along the top edge of the stocking like a fluffy cuff, placing them close to each other so they fit well together.

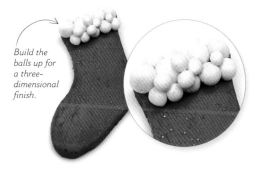

Build the balls up for a three-dimensional finish.

6 Position a few white balls on top of the first batch so that no red clay can be seen.

7 Mould a small white heart about 5 mm (³⁄₁₆ in) long, and place this in position underneath the white balls.

8 Use a cocktail stick to guide an eyepin into the top of the stocking, behind the white balls. Bake the charm, following the clay manufacturer's instructions.

Stocking fillers
The stocking shape is easy to adapt and personalize for a particular recipient.

Shape a blade from silver clay for an ice-skate stocking.

Gift-wrapped box

These adorable little charms make the perfect present. Make these easily with only a few steps and techniques, including accurate slicing and a little bit of tricky shaping. Why not make a birthday charm bracelet for a friend's special day?

Tools & materials

● Mauve clay
● Orange clay

☑ Rolling pin
☑ Blade
☑ Cocktail stick
☑ Eyepin

Actual size & dimensions

A Height 10 mm (³⁄₈ in)
B Width 10 mm (³⁄₈ in)
C Depth 10 mm (³⁄₈ in)

1 Use a rolling pin to roll a thick piece of conditioned mauve clay to about 7.5 mm (⁵⁄₁₆ in) deep. Try to keep the clay level at the top. Use a blade to even up the edges.

2 Cut the clay into a cube shape, making sure that the width and length of the clay are of a similar size to the depth. Make sure the cube is an even shape and, if not, use the blade to make corrections.

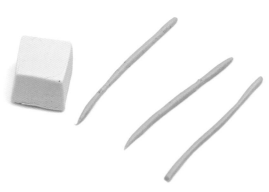

Check that the ribbon is positioned centrally on the box.

3 Roll three strings of orange clay about 3 cm (1¼ in) long and 1 mm (¹⁄₃₂ in) wide. Roll these on the work surface and try to make their thicknesses consistent. These will form the ribbons for the box.

4 Wrap the first string over one face of the cube, across the top and back down the opposite side. Try to make sure that the ribbon is in the middle of the face and not slanted or too far to one side.

Skill level: ●●●

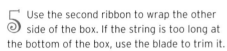

Position the bow slightly off-centre, so that the eyepin can be centrally inserted in the next step.

5 Use the second ribbon to wrap the other side of the box. If the string is too long at the bottom of the box, use the blade to trim it.

6 Use the final string to create a figure-of-eight and fix together in the centre with a tiny ball of the same colour. Use a cocktail stick to help position this on top of the gift box but a little off-centre, so that there is room behind it for the eyepin.

What's the occasion?
Thread cord through your bracelet to give it a little extra colour, then attach your gift boxes every few links.

7 Use the cocktail stick to insert the eyepin into the centre of the charm. This will ensure that it hangs straight and will mainly be hidden by the bow. Bake the charm, following the clay manufacturer's instructions.

Present perfect
Make these little presents in coordinating colours or different shades for a little variety and to suit the occasion!

2

Materials, tools and techniques

This chapter looks in detail at the equipment and techniques you need to create polymer clay charms, and backs up the information given with each project.

Polymer clays

Oven-bake polymer clay is a versatile modelling material that is soft and malleable until it is baked, when it becomes hard. It consists of pigments and PVC particles, bound together by a plasticizer to form a clay-like material that can be modelled, moulded, sculpted, blended, textured and embellished. The beauty of working with polymer clay is that the basics are quickly mastered, even if you are new to the material.

There are many types of polymer clay. Brands vary slightly in firmness and strength before and after baking, so test them to see which ones you prefer. Clay manufacturers also make varnishes for use with their clays.

Coloured clay
Polymer clay is available in a huge range of opaque colours, and these can be mixed together to create an even larger colour palette.

Metallic and special-effect colours
Some metallic clays contain glitter for a sparkly effect, while others contain mica particles for creating mica shift and pearlescent effects. Special-effect clays include imitation stone and gem colours, as well as fluorescent colours.

Translucent clay
Translucent (or porcelain) clay is colourless. It can be used on its own or mixed with coloured clay. Ready-mixed translucent colours are also available. Mixing translucent with metallic mica clays helps to spread out the mica particles to create more sparkle (mica clays on their own have a satin metallic finish). After baking, quench pieces containing translucent clay in ice water to enhance the translucency.

Liquid clay
Liquid clay is available as a translucent medium and in various colours, as well as in different clarities, with some being more glass-like than others. It can be used for gluing clay to clay, for softening standard clay and for simulating glazes. It is also a versatile medium in its own right, and can be baked in moulds, spread out to create sheets and used for image transfers.

Varnish
It is not necessary to varnish baked clay to protect it; instead, varnishes are used to protect surface finishes such as paints and powders, as well as for the look of the varnish itself. You can use a varnish manufactured especially for polymer clay work, or any clear-drying water-based varnish. Varnishes are available in matt, satin and gloss finishes.

SAFETY NOTE
Polymer clay is nontoxic; it gives off a slight smell during baking, but this is not harmful. However, if you accidentally overheat the clay, it will burn. Burning plastic can give off fumes that may be toxic. If this happens, switch off the oven immediately (do not open it) and ventilate the room well. Leave the area until the fumes have cleared. Although polymer clay is nontoxic, it is not food-safe, so it should not be used for making vessels for eating or drinking.

Metallic clay

Fluorescent clay

Coloured clay

Translucent clay

Eyeshadow powder

Decorating equipment

Polymer clay combines beautifully with all kinds of other materials, from paints and inks to powders, resins and even dried herbs. The following materials are known to be stable when used with polymer clay, and can enhance and embellish your work in hundreds of ways.

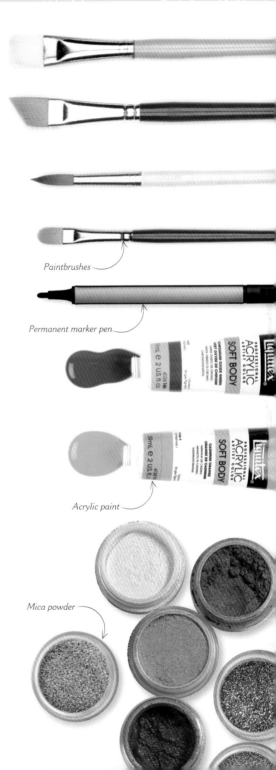

Paintbrushes

Permanent marker pen

Acrylic paint

Mica powder

Pastels and powders

Chalk pastels can be mixed into raw clay or applied to the surface with a brush, fingertip or sponge. They can also be mixed into liquid clay or varnish and painted onto baked clay before rebaking to heat-set the colour. Grate the stick of chalk pastel using a piece of coarse sandpaper and store the grated powder in a jar.

Finely ground mica powders can be found in a huge range of colours, from metallics to iridescent colours, and are used in the same way as chalk pastels.

Beauty products such as eyeshadows (which have mica powders in them also) and blushers can be used as alternatives, as well as powdered unfired china glazes, childrens' coloured chalks and oil pastels.

Acrylic paint

This is the best paint to use with polymer clay. Choose a good-quality artist's acrylic paint that dries on the surface of both raw and baked clay (some paints and inks never dry on raw clay). The advantage of this is that you can manipulate the clay after the paint has dried without marring the design. You can even run

the clay through a pasta machine. To be sure of the paint adhering to the surface when applied to baked clay, put the piece back into the oven at 95°C (200°F) for 15 minutes. Allow to cool before touching.

Acrylic paints come in both opaque and metallic colours and can be mixed with a gel medium to create a translucent paint.

Alcohol ink

These concentrated ink colours can be used to tint raw or baked polymer clay to create beautifully rich, jewel-like colours.

Paintbrushes

Use artists' paintbrushes to apply powders, paints and inks.

Permanent marker pens

Permanent marker pens can be used to draw onto baked clay to add final, and fine, detailing. Not all pens will work with polymer clay, so you need to test them first. Be aware that, even though some pens say they are permanent, they may bleed into the surface of the clay and look fuzzy over time.

Alcohol ink

Findings and jewellery

Findings are small metal components that are used to complete a piece of jewellery and, in this case, to attach your charms to your jewellery. At the most basic level you will need eyepins and jump rings, and probably a chain, but will no doubt want to experiment with other findings and different styles of jewellery as you make more charms. You will also need wire cutters and pliers to enable you to work with the findings.

Attaching charms

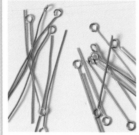

Eyepins
Eyepins are straight wires with a loop at one end. The straight wire is inserted into the charm, and the looped end used to attach the charm to the jewellery.

Headpins
Headpins are straight wires up to 7.5 cm (3 in) long, with a flattened end to keep beads from falling off. They are used for dangly beaded earrings.

Jump rings
Jump rings are used to connect charms to chains or to other pieces of jewellery.

Split rings
Like key rings with double rings of wire, split rings are stronger and more secure than jump rings. They are also more difficult to open.

Pliers

Wire cutters
Where necessary, use wire cutters to cut an eyepin to size, remembering to leave extra for the loop if the pin is reinserted after baking (see opposite). Buy a pair with neat, pointed ends to cut close to the work.

Jewellery

Chains
Chains come in different designs and are used for bracelets and necklaces. Attach charms or beads to chains using jump rings.

Waxed cotton cord
Various types of cord make an interesting alternative to chains. Attach charms to cord using jump rings in the usual way.

Fishhook wires
Fishhook wires hook through the pierced ear. The loop is opened like a jump ring to hook onto the charm's eyepin.

Brooch backs, bar pins and earring posts
Use epoxy glue to attach clay charms to findings such as brooch backs, bar pins and earring posts.

Round-nose pliers
Round-nose pliers are used for forming round loops in wire, and pliers can also be useful when opening and closing jump rings.

Fasteners

Spring-end crimps
Spring-end crimps are used to attach cord to a fastener.

Toggles
Toggle or ring-and-bar clasps are available in a wide choice of styles, sizes and weights. The T-bar must be able to pass through the ring, turn and lie flat.

Magnetic clasps
Magnetic clasps are useful for people with arthritis, but they are not as readily available as other fasteners.

Screw clasps
Screw clasps screw shut and are available with or without a loop.

Lobster claw clasps
Lobster claw or trigger clasps have a hinged bar that is operated with a spring lever to keep it closed.

Threading a pin after baking

Some charms are more stable if the eyepin is fitted after baking. This is specified in the relevant projects, and a hole will always be made in the charm before baking. The technique for fixing an eyepin in this way can also be applied to threading beads onto a headpin.

1 Thread the baked charm or beads onto the eye- or headpin, leaving one end of the wire exposed.

2 Use your fingers to bend the end of the wire 90°, then cut the wire with wire cutters, leaving about 1 cm (3/8 in) or enough to make a loop.

Attaching a jump ring

1 With a pair of pliers in each hand, open the jump ring by twisting the ends sideways. Thread the jump ring through the charm's eyepin and onto the jewellery, then close the ring by twisting the ends back towards each other.

3 Grasp the end of the wire with round-nose pliers, and turn the pliers to form a loop. Check that the loop is centred over the beads or charm.

Attaching spring-end crimps

Cut the end of the cord and insert it into the crimp. Squeeze the end of the crimp with pliers to crimp the metal onto the cord. Use a jump ring to attach a clasp to the crimp.

Making equipment

Polymer clay is easily shaped in your hands, and to begin with the only piece of equipment you will need is a smooth and shiny surface. A rolling pin and blade will come in very handy, and as you start to make more varied projects you can add to your collection of tools as appropriate.

Straight craft knife blade

Ripple blade

Slicer blade

Craft knife

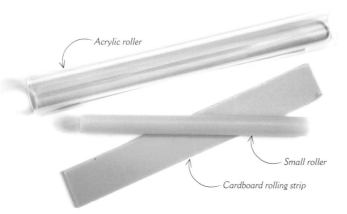

Acrylic roller

Small roller

Cardboard rolling strip

Cutting tools
Long thin blades, called tissue blades or slicer blades, are used for cutting straight lines and for slicing canes. Ripple blades are used for slicing clay to make special effects. A craft knife with a curved blade can also be a useful cutting tool.

Rolling pins and strips
A clear acrylic rolling pin is nonstick and allows you to see the clay through it. A small rolling pin is useful for miniatures. Rolling strips are simply strips of card or wood of a required thickness, and are used to keep your rolling even.

Bathroom tile

Ballpoint refill with cone tip

Tapestry needle

Working surface
The surface you work on with polymer clay should be wipeable and smooth. A melamine chopping board works well, while ceramic tiles are useful for working and baking on. Perspex and glass also make ideal working surfaces.

Cutters
You can use brass cutters with plungers to push out the clay shape, as well as cutters from polymer clay suppliers, kitchen equipment shops and cake-decorating suppliers.

Texturing tools
The cocktail stick is often the first choice of texturing tool, used to make dots, lines and the crumble cake texture. Other improvised tools for texturing clay include a tapestry needle, a ballpoint refill (dried up) with a cone tip and a ball-headed pin. Rubber, wooden and metal stamps also work beautifully with polymer clay: choose stamps that have clear-cut designs with good relief.

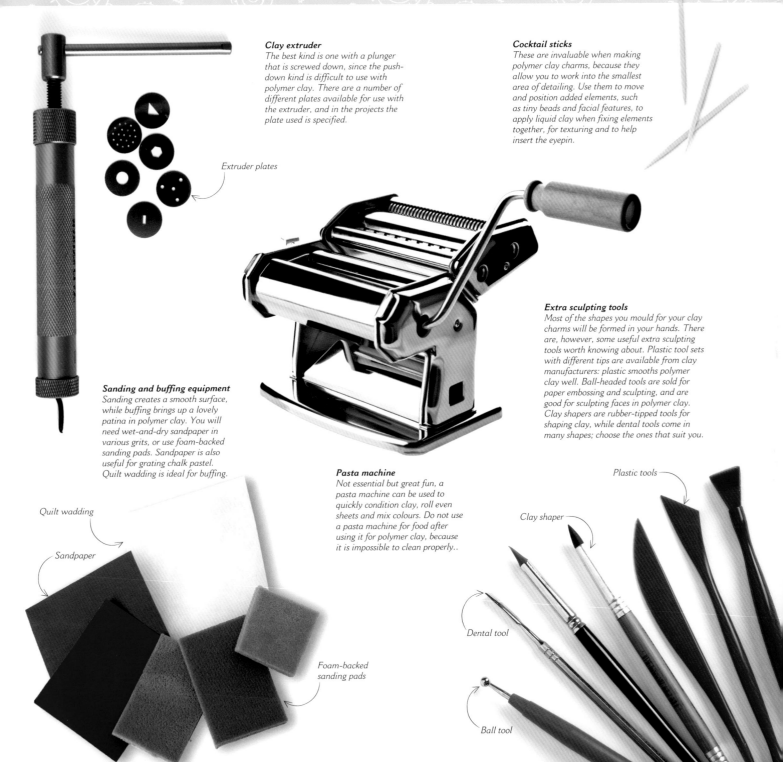

Clay extruder
The best kind is one with a plunger that is screwed down, since the push-down kind is difficult to use with polymer clay. There are a number of different plates available for use with the extruder, and in the projects the plate used is specified.

Extruder plates

Cocktail sticks
These are invaluable when making polymer clay charms, because they allow you to work into the smallest area of detailing. Use them to move and position added elements, such as tiny beads and facial features, to apply liquid clay when fixing elements together, for texturing and to help insert the eyepin.

Sanding and buffing equipment
Sanding creates a smooth surface, while buffing brings up a lovely patina in polymer clay. You will need wet-and-dry sandpaper in various grits, or use foam-backed sanding pads. Sandpaper is also useful for grating chalk pastel. Quilt wadding is ideal for buffing.

Quilt wadding

Sandpaper

Foam-backed sanding pads

Extra sculpting tools
Most of the shapes you mould for your clay charms will be formed in your hands. There are, however, some useful extra sculpting tools worth knowing about. Plastic tool sets with different tips are available from clay manufacturers: plastic smooths polymer clay well. Ball-headed tools are sold for paper embossing and sculpting, and are good for sculpting faces in polymer clay. Clay shapers are rubber-tipped tools for shaping clay, while dental tools come in many shapes; choose the ones that suit you.

Pasta machine
Not essential but great fun, a pasta machine can be used to quickly condition clay, roll even sheets and mix colours. Do not use a pasta machine for food after using it for polymer clay, because it is impossible to clean properly..

Plastic tools

Clay shaper

Dental tool

Ball tool

Conditioning clay

Polymer clay must be conditioned before use, even if it is a new block. Conditioning makes the crumbly clay malleable and easier to work, and removes tiny pockets of air that, when heated, can leave an uneven surface on the baked clay.

Hand conditioning

You can use the warmth of your hands to soften and condition polymer clay. Do not try to condition more than about a quarter of a 56 g (2 oz) pack at a time, unless you have very strong hands.

FIRM CLAY BY HAND

Clay that is not new out of the packet may be firm and crumbly. Knead small pieces of the firm clay with your fingers, warming it as you do so. As soon as any crumbling diminishes, roll the clay into a log, folding and repeating until it becomes pliable. Now combine the smaller pieces into a larger log and repeat until the clay is conditioned.

1 Open the packet of clay and cut off several small pieces.

3 Roll the clay between the palms of your hands to form a log.

2 Squeeze the pieces of clay together with your fingers.

4 Fold the shape in half, then roll it between your palms again. Repeat this process a few times until the clay is well conditioned (see right).

Checking for good condition

1 To check that the clay is properly conditioned, shape a piece into a log with a diameter of 12.5 mm (½ in), and bend it in half. If it cracks, it needs more conditioning.

2 If the shape bends, it is properly conditioned.

Good conditioning
Clay that will be used in an extruder, for example to make this long thread, must be really well conditioned.

Machine conditioning

A pasta machine will condition polymer clay rapidly, and is a useful investment if you make a lot of charms.

1 Use a blade to cut the clay from the block into sheets 6 mm (¹⁄₄ in) thick or less. Set the pasta machine on the widest setting and pass each sheet through the machine.

2 Press two sheets together and pass through again, repeating until all the sheets are combined into one large sheet. Now fold the sheet in half and, placing the fold vertically to avoid trapping air in the clay, pass through again. Repeat as necessary until the clay is conditioned. Most clays need a maximum of ten passes through a pasta machine to condition them.

Storing clay

* Until polymer clay is baked, it can be reused over and over, and has a shelf life of many years. The clay will slowly harden in the pack as the plasticizer evaporates, but if stored carefully it will remain usable for years.

* Store opened clay in a dustproof container, such as a metal tin or a polythene box.

* The plasticizer in the clay will react with some types of plastic. To counteract this, wrap the clay in baking parchment.

* Baking parchment is also useful for keeping sheets of clay and different colours separate.

* Store the clay in a cool place away from heat and sunlight - polymer clay starts to bake at very low temperatures and can even start to cure if left on a window ledge.

FIRM CLAY BY MACHINE

If, when conditioning clay that has been kept in storage, the clay is firm and crumbles a lot on the first pass through the machine, press the cut-off sheet with your fingers to warm and thin it before passing it through again.

Colour mixing

Mixing clay colours is like mixing paint. With a few basic colours you can make and match a host of other colours. Mix in a touch of black to reduce the brightness of a coloured clay, or mix in an abundance of white to create pastel colours.

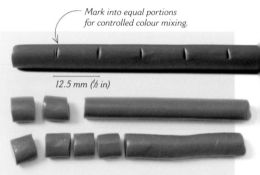

Marbling
You can use clay that has been partially colour mixed for a marbled effect, or keep mixing until a single colour is achieved.

The intensity of ready-made, shop-bought colours varies enormously. Some, such as red, are overpowering in a mix, so use them sparingly. Tint translucent clay by adding a small amount of coloured clay.

Combining colours

A good way to mix colours is to cut your two clays into equally sized small portions, and combine them in differing proportions, depending on the shade you want to achieve. Remember to keep a note of the colour proportions you use.

Mixing small amounts of coloured clay at a time can be useful for carrying out colour tests. It is quick and easy and guarantees that you won't end up with a very large amount of a disappointing colour.

Mixing colours

Roll, twist and fold clay by hand to mix colours.

Mark into equal portions for controlled colour mixing.

12.5 mm (½ in)

1 Roll two clays into logs with a diameter of about 12.5 mm (½ in). Use a blade to cut along the shapes at intervals of 12.5 mm (½ in).

2 In this example, two portions of blue clay are mixed with four portions of pink clay. Roll the clays into individual thinner snake shapes and lay the shapes together.

3 Roll and twist the two snakes together to form a single log. The colours will begin to marble together.

4 Fold the log in half and roll and twist again.

5 Continue to roll, twist, and fold until the colours have mixed thoroughly. If you dislike the colour, add another piece of one of the clays and roll and twist again to mix the colours.

The two colours have blended completely.

TIPS

* Light colours are easy to ruin, so mix your light colours before the dark ones. Use wet hand wipes to keep hands, tools and work surface clean.
* Newly mixed colours that don't work are not wasted. Use them as the centre of a charm that will be wrapped, such as the egg on pages 106–107.
* Warm clay is easier to mix, but do not try to warm it other than naturally between the hands.

The Skinner technique

The Skinner blend was developed by Judith Skinner, who found that different-coloured clays could be combined together using a pasta machine so that they blended smoothly from one solid colour to another. This technique has been used by polymer clay artists in a wide variety of ways ever since. Before making a Skinner blend, see what the colours will look like when mixed together. To do this, mix equal small portions of the two colours by hand. Skinner blends can be made of two or more colours.

1 Choose two different-coloured clays and roll a sheet of each on the thickest setting of a pasta machine. Use a blade to cut each sheet into a square with a width that is just short of the width of the pasta machine. Make a diagonal cut across each square, 2.5 cm (1 in) in from each corner. Dividing the sheets in this way will mean that there is unmixed colour at each end of the blend.

2 Form a new square by positioning a triangle of one colour next to the corresponding triangle in the second colour. Put the other two triangles to one side.

3 Fold the two coloured sheets back on themselves and press them together.

4 Place the folded edge of the clay in the pasta machine and roll through on the thickest setting.

5 Fold the clay sheet in half again and roll it through the pasta machine on the thickest setting, fold first.

6 Continue to fold and roll the clay another ten to fifteen times. Gradually the streaked colours will blend together, creating another colour – in this case orange. The clay sheet will become misshapen, but this is natural.

7 By the final roll through the pasta machine the colours will form a continuous blend from one edge to the other.

Rolling sheets

Rolling polymer clay into sheets is the starting point of many projects. For the projects in this book the clay was rolled by hand, but using a pasta machine is an alternative way of rolling quickly and evenly.

Hand rolling

You can roll polymer clay into sheets using a smooth rolling pin. To achieve an even thickness, you can roll with the help of rolling strips of the desired thickness.

Machine rolling

Air bubbles can be a problem when rolling sheets in a pasta machine, especially with clay that is being reused, because air pockets may have become trapped inside.

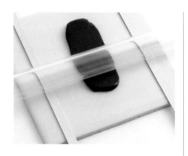

1 Use your hands to flatten a piece of conditioned clay into a pancake. Lay the clay on a smooth surface and place a rolling strip on either side. Roll over the clay firmly with a rolling pin until the clay sheet is the thickness of the strips.

2 The rolled clay sheet will stick to the surface below, but it is easy enough to peel off the sheet unless you roll very thinly. For very thin sheets, or for rolling clay that is relatively soft and sticky, place the clay pancake between two sheets of greaseproof paper as you roll.

1 Set the pasta machine to the required thickness. Fold the conditioned clay in half and insert it into the rollers with the fold at the side to avoid trapping air bubbles in the clay. Wind smoothly and evenly without stopping while the clay is between the rollers.

2 If air bubbles appear in the surface of the clay, fold the worst bubbles to the outside and roll again, making sure that you place the fold at the side. Repeat, so that the bubbles work to the surface and disperse.

Squaring the sheet

To stop the edges of the sheet from becoming ragged as you roll them, press one edge of the sheet against the side of the pasta machine as you roll to straighten it. Fold the sheet, rotate it, press another edge against the side and so on.

TIP

Some projects require the thinnest possible sheet of clay. The last setting on most pasta machines usually cockles the clay (shown right), so get to know your machine and find the thinnest sheet it will roll to. To roll very thin sheets of clay, roll as thinly as possible on the machine, then lay the sheet on a piece of nonstick greaseproof paper and roll even thinner by hand.

Using an extruder

Using an extruder is a great way to make uniform fine strands or a specific shape that is even throughout. Softened clay is inserted into the barrel of the extruder and a plunger is twisted to press the clay down and extrude it through a shaped plate at the end.

TIPS

* Always use warmed and softened clay. Hard clay may show stress marks or tears when extruded and is much harder to push out.
* Keep the extruder as clean as possible; wipe out the inside with alcohol or wet wipes.
* Spray the inside of the extruder with silicone furniture polish to make it easier to clean.

Making extrusions

Always check that the extruder is clean before you use it, to avoid disappointing results.

1 Condition the clay well, since softer clay is easier to extrude. Undo the end of the barrel and insert the softened clay. Place a plate of your choice on the end of the extruder and screw down the holding collar.

2 Wind the handle; the clay will extrude from the plate. Keep winding until all of the clay has been extruded. Use the extrusions fairly soon after making them, so that they retain their flexibility and do not stiffen as they become cool.

Striped extrusions

Press logs of contrasting colours together and insert them into the barrel. The resulting extrusion will have stripes of colour that grade subtly into one another.

Wrapped extrusions

Fill the barrel with clay in one colour, then add 12.5 mm (½ in) of another colour. Extrude the clay; after the first inch or so, the extrusion will have an interior colour of the first clay wrapped in a shell of the second colour.

Shape it
The numerous plates available allow you to extrude many different shapes of clay.

Experiment with different-shaped plates.

We use this plate for the patterned egg on pages 106–107.

Shaping clay

Simple shapes, such as balls and snakes, are the building blocks of many polymer clay charms. Cutters are also frequently used with sheets of clay, while a repertoire of extra shapes is useful too.

Log

Snake

String

Smooth disks

Shape conditioned clay into a ball between the palms of your hands. Place the ball on the tile and press down with the pad of your finger.

Scalloped disks

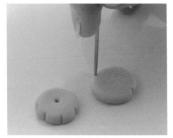

Press the side of a needle into the disks at even intervals all around.

Egg shapes

Roll your upper hand back and forth lightly over a ball of clay to form an egg shape.

Teardrop

Press the side of your upper palm onto one side of a ball and roll it back and forth to point that side.

Rolling a log, snake and string

1 Roll a ball of well-conditioned clay between the palms of your hands. Place the ball on the work surface and shape it into a thick log by rolling it on the work surface with your hands.

2 Make the shape thinner by rolling the clay backward and forward under your hand on the work surface. Use both hands when both will fit on the shape. As you roll, move your hands towards the ends of the clay. Gradually the clay log will get longer and thinner as it becomes a snake.

3 Depending on the thickness of shape you require, you can continue rolling the clay until it makes a thin string. Use the fingertips of one hand to roll the clay, at the same time raising the thick end of the clay up with your other hand, to take up slack as the string gets longer. Carefully pull the thinner portion out and away so you make a very thin string.

Leaves

1 Start by shaping a small teardrop, then flatten the clay to create a leaf shape.

2 Use a cocktail stick to press a line down the centre of the shape. Pinch the base of the leaf so that it curves slightly.

Bows

1 Use a rolling pin to roll a thin sheet of well-conditioned clay about 2 mm (1/16 in) thick, 2 cm (3/4 in) long and 1 cm (3/8 in) wide. Use a blade to trim the edges so that they are clean and straight. Cut each corner diagonally to look neater at the end.

2 Fold the two ends under the middle of the clay rectangle and pinch in the centre. Finally, wrap a small strip of clay around the centre of the bow.

Using cutters

1 Roll out a sheet of clay to the thickness required and press the sheet lightly onto a ceramic tile so that it adheres. You can brush the surface of the clay lightly with talcum powder or cornflour to prevent the cutter from sticking in the clay.

2 Press the cutter down firmly into the clay, until it contacts the tile all around. The natural stickiness of the clay should stop the pieces from being removed with the cutter; if they dislodge, press the sheet down a little.

3 Remove the cutter and pull away the scrap clay. You can bake the cut-out pieces on the tile to avoid distorting them while they are soft if this suits the project. If you need to manipulate them while they are soft, slide a blade under each one to free it from the tile.

Using templates

Lay the template on a sheet of clay that has been pressed lightly onto a tile to stick it down. Cut around the template with a craft knife; remove the excess clay and the template.

Leaves
Leaves are a useful motif for decorating other charms.

Caning and stacking

Polymer clay canes are created in the same way as a stick of holiday rock, and slices from the soft cane can be used to create or decorate all kinds of charms.

Spiral canes can be shaped into triangular or square canes. Pinch along the cane to form the angles. Use a rolling pin along the sides to smooth out the pinch marks.

Spiral cane

Use contrasting-coloured clays to clearly show the spiral pattern. Alternatively, make a spiral with a Skinner blend sheet (see page 129) for a cane with colour that changes smoothly from the outside to the inside.

1 Roll out two sheets of clay. Use a blade to cut both sheets into rectangles of the same size, and place one sheet on top of the other. Use a rolling pin to smooth the sheets and expel any air pockets.

2 Cut both short ends of the sheet at an angle to reveal the lower sheet of clay.

3 Using your fingertips, roll the sheet up to make a tight spiral. Continue to roll to the end of the sheet, making sure that the inside sheet is completely covered by the outside sheet. Roll the cane on the work surface with both hands to make it more compact.

4 Use a blade to slice down into the cane and reveal the spiral pattern.

This strawberry decoration is also sliced from a cane (see page 137).

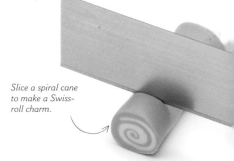

Slice a spiral cane to make a Swiss-roll charm.

Reducing a cane

'Reducing' is the process of stretching a large patterned cane. Some polymer clay artists make elaborate canes that are several inches in diameter before they reduce them. To make a range of cane sizes, cut chunks off the cane at different stages of reduction. Wherever you cut a slice from a reduced cane the image will be exactly the same, with no loss of definition. Large canes tend to twist as they are reduced, so you may need to make a registration mark along the full length of the cane to help keep it straight as you reduce it: use a very thin line of translucent clay, because this will disappear when the clay is baked.

1 Once rolled, leave the cane to rest so that all the clay reaches the same temperature. Begin to reduce the cane by pinching around the middle with your fingertips, to form an hourglass shape. Work your fingers towards the ends of the cane, pinching and rotating as you go. When reducing a larger cane, the ends may disappear inside the cane or the clay on the outside may run out as it becomes warmer and softer from handling. This is normal.

2 Pinch around the end of the cane. Keep alternating from one end of the cane to the other. Once you have reduced the cane to the size you require, roll the cane on the work surface to smooth out any pinch marks. You can cut chunks or slices off the cane at any point during the reduction, to keep for later use, before you reduce the cane further.

Bull's-eye cane

This simple cane demonstrates the basics of making a round bull's-eye cane. Once you have mastered the basic technique you can use it and adapt it to create other designs.

1 Roll the first clay colour into a log. Use a rolling pin to roll the second clay colour into a sheet that is large enough to wrap around the log. Lay the log on one edge of the sheet.

2 Roll the log up in the sheet until the first edge of the sheet meets the sheet again, where it will make a slight mark on the clay surface. Unroll a little and use a blade to cut across the sheet along the mark.

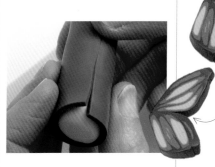

3 The edges of the sheet should meet in a butt joint. Smooth the joint with a thumb or finger. You can now reduce the cane (roll it to make it smaller in diameter and much longer) and slice it as necessary, or use it in an extruder.

This complex-looking butterfly wing began life as a bull's-eye cane.

Wrap a log in several sheets of clay in contrasting colours and of different thicknesses to make a more complex bull's-eye cane.

Striped cane

Striped canes can be made using rolled sheets of any thickness, and the stripes show best when contrasting-coloured clays are used. Thin slices from these canes can then be used as veneers, or thick slices can be cut to form solid beads.

1 Roll out sheets of two contrasting colours. Using a blade, cut each sheet in half and stack the halves to make double-thickness sheets of each colour. Cut each sheet in half again and trim into rectangles. Stack the sheets, alternating the colours to make a striped cane.

2 Using a rolling pin, smooth the stack to expel any air pockets, then cut your slices.

Checked cane

Stack these slices, alternating the colours of each layer, to form a chessboard pattern. Use the rolling pin to smooth the cane and compress the layers.

A striped cane is used for this bunting charm.

Lime cane

This little fruit cane can be used to decorate cakes and tarts, or even on beads. Simply bake, slice and use whenever you need. Try the technique using translucent green clay wrapped in yellow for a lemon, or use pink for a grapefruit.

1 Use a blade to cut a thick circle of conditioned green clay into eight equal segments.

2 Use a rolling pin to roll a thin sheet of white clay and cut strips to the same length as your green sections. Place a white strip between each green section. Trim any excess white clay.

3 Wrap the whole shape with a sheet of white clay followed by a sheet of dark green clay. Pinch out the shape to reduce the cane to about 5 mm (³/₁₆ in).

Strawberry cane

This variation on a round fruit cane provides strawberry slices that can be used to decorate various charms. As with the lime cane, simply bake the cane and slice whenever needed.

1 Use a rolling pin to roll a thin sheet of conditioned white clay about 2 mm (¹/₁₆ in) thick, 1 cm (³/₈ in) wide and 2 cm (³/₄ in) long. Position this on top of a thicker layer of light pink clay and place this directly on top of an even thicker layer of bright pink clay. Smooth the layers together.

2 Cut this strip into ten sections and place a thin strip of white clay between each section. Smooth the sections back together.

3 Roll a snake of white clay and wrap half of it with light pink clay. Bend the strip made in Step 2 over the light pink clay.

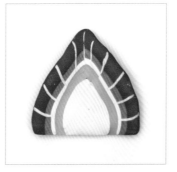

4 Pinch the top to create the distinctive strawberry shape. Pinch the shape to reduce the cane to about 5 mm (³/₁₆ in), or to your preferred size.

Baking

Baking, or 'curing', is an essential part of all polymer clay work. Heat causes the polyvinyl particles in the clay to polymerize, making the clay hard and strong. Under-baking will result in weakened clay and beads that may crack.

Most clay brands recommend baking at 130°C (266°F) for about 30 minutes, but baking for longer, or rebaking several times, does not seem to harm the clay. Always check the packet for baking instructions as temperatures and baking times can vary between brands.

Place the items on a baking tray on the middle shelf of the oven for even heating. If you are baking tall pieces or think that your oven heats unevenly, then cover the tray with a 'tent' of aluminium foil.

Temperature and duration

Opinions about temperatures and baking times vary enormously, so experiment with the oven settings and the thermometer to find out what suits you and the charms you are baking. It is advisable to purchase an oven thermometer to help you check the oven settings.

Baking surface

Bake polymer clay pieces on a baking tray, an ovenproof dish, a ceramic tile or a piece of glass. The low oven temperatures will not affect these surfaces. Cover a metal baking surface with greaseproof paper or ordinary paper, which stops the clay from scorching where it touches the metal. Do the same to avoid a shiny surface where the clay rests on the baking surface, or bake the pieces on a bed of baking powder, which simply brushes off when hardened.

Baking sheets

To bake an extremely flat, even sheet of clay, place the sheet between two sheets of greaseproof paper and lay this on a tile, with an

Baking sheets of clay
Sandwich the clay sheet between two sheets of greaseproof paper, with a tile on top and one below.

upturned tile over it to hold it down. Bake for the usual amount of time plus about ten minutes to allow for the tiles to heat through. This ensures that the sheet is completely flat and smooth after baking.

Baking charms

To stop charms and beads from rolling around or sticking to each other on the baking tray, there are several ways you can separate and support them.

Charms can be placed on a bed of polyester fibrefill. The texture of this material will not impress on the charms and the temperature necessary for baking polymer clay is not high enough to melt the polyester fibres.

Bake flat charms on paper to prevent them from getting shiny spots from contact with metal, glass or ceramic tiles. However, bear in mind that placing round beads on paper may leave a round, flat mark on the bead. Small

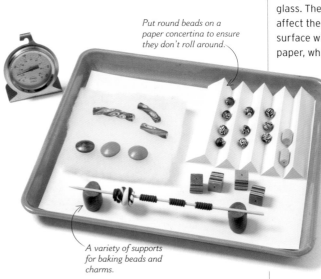

Put round beads on a paper concertina to ensure they don't roll around.

A variety of supports for baking beads and charms.

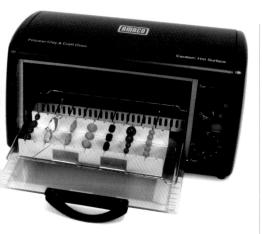

Polymer clay oven
A worktop polymer clay oven could be a good investment if you make lots of charms. You can even buy special baking trays to suit your needs. Here, a designer has set up the tray with her own polymer clay beads ready to bake.

round balls can be baked on a folded paper concertina to stop them from rolling around.

Supports

Beads with a thread hole can be threaded onto a wire or bamboo skewer and supported at each end on a stand. This method is useful if the beads are textured. (If the cooled beads are difficult to remove from the skewer, put the skewer and beads back into a hot oven for a few moments and remove from the skewer while they are still warm.)

To make the stands, use a scrap clay shaped into thick, short sausage shapes. Stand each shape on its end and use a bamboo skewer or similar tool to press across the clay to make a channel. Stand the two pieces upright to bake.

You can make these stands any height you wish, so that large beads can be raised above the base of the baking tray as they bake.

Ovens

You can use a household oven to bake your charms, but this is not recommended. If you make charms on a regular basis, invest in a small worktop oven dedicated to polymer clay use only. Many polymer clay artists use a toaster or convection oven. A fan-assisted oven ensures that the heat is circulated more evenly throughout the oven. If you do use a household oven, make a tent' out of aluminium foil or use a lidded casserole or baking dish to prevent the plasticizer residue from being deposited on the oven walls.

You may notice a slight smell during baking; this is normal and harmless. However, it is sensible always to ventilate the workroom since when clay overheats the fumes are unpleasant and possibly toxic. If possible, bake in a separate room to where you work.

Never try to bake your charms in a microwave oven.

Cooling

It does not seem to matter whether charms are left to cool slowly in the oven or removed while hot, although cooling in the oven can be a useful way to toughen beads. Once baked, polymer clay remains pliable until it has cooled. This is a useful feature if you want to bend pieces and 'set' them to a new shape while holding them under cold running water.

Finishing

Polymer clay does not have to be sealed for protection or to make it stronger, so the finishing techniques of sanding, buffing or varnishing are, on the whole, used for effect rather than out of necessity.

A glossy varnish gives this charm a characteristic glaze effect.

Sanding and buffing

Sanding and buffing can be used to give baked clay an attractive sheen and to maximize the transparency of translucent clay: translucent polymer clay is much more transparent when the surface is buffed and sanded.

Sanding

Hold the baked polymer clay piece under a gently running tap. Lukewarm water helps to soften the clay and makes sanding quicker. Sand first with a coarse sandpaper or sanding pad to remove the major blemishes, then progress through to medium, then fine. The running water helps to prevent the sandpaper or sanding pad from clogging.

Buffing by hand

The sanded surface will look dusty and pale in colour and needs to be buffed. A good firm rub with quilt wadding, a stiff cotton fabric such as denim or even a pair of nylon tights, will buff the surface to a shiny patina.

* You can use either wet-and-dry sandpaper or foam-backed sanding pads.

* To get a really good, smooth finish, you will need three types: coarse (300-400 grit); medium (800-1000 grit); and fine (1200-1400 grit).

* Fine steel wool is also useful for smoothing baked polymer clay; use it instead of the coarse-grit sandpaper.

This marbled bead has been buffed to a high sheen.

Finishing touch
As these beads show, varnish choice will depend on the effect you wish to achieve.

Plain baked bead   *Matt varnish*   *Satin varnish*   *Gloss varnish*

Varnishing

Baked polymer clay does not gain added strength or durability with a layer of varnish. Instead, varnish is used to provide a gloss to the surface, or to protect paint or other applied finishes.

Apply varnish directly to the clay surface after baking. To prevent beading (when a water-based varnish will not stick properly on the clay and gathers in droplets on the surface), brush the surface of the baked clay with alcohol and allow to dry before varnishing. Apply a second coat of varnish when the first is fully dry to achieve a higher shine.

Some polymer clays can develop bleeding in the clay surrounding a painted area some time after the paint was applied. To avoid this, coat the clay with a matt varnish before painting, then seal with a top coat of varnish when the paint is dry. Allow to dry thoroughly before applying the top coat of varnish; this will avoid any clouding of the varnish.

Varnishing charms

Apply a coat of varnish with a paintbrush. Small pieces are difficult to hold when varnishing, so pin them down with the point of a large, blunt-ended needle as you brush on the varnish.

Varnishing beads

Thread beads temporarily onto a piece of wire to enable you to varnish several beads at a time without them rolling about. Bend a hook in one end of the wire to hang it up until the beads are dry.

Varnish will protect the alcohol ink used to decorate these charms.

Index

Credits

Key: b = bottom, c = centre, l= left, r = right, t = top

Quarto would like to thank Nadia Michaux for supplying the charms on pages 10tr, 21b, 29b, 30b, 33b, 41b, 51b, 55b, 59b, 63b, 65b, 67b, 69b, 71b (cat and bear), 72b, 75b, 81b, 84b, 87b, 89b, 107b, 109b, 111b, 113b, 115b, 140t
www.littlestsweetshop.com

Quarto would like to thank the following for kindly supplying images for inclusion in the book:
∗ Amaco (American Art Clay Company) 139t *www. amaco.com*
∗ Kat Davies 11bl *www.etsy.com/shop/ LavenderandBees*
∗ Sue Heaser 10bl/c *www.sueheaser.com*
∗ Lin Javalera 11tl/c/tr *www.sweetestcharms.com*
∗ Sherri Kellberg 10tl/c *www.etsy.com/shop/ beadazzleme*
∗ Paulina Negrete Marin 11br *www.elartedepau.com*
∗ Petrina Marie Pigrum 11c *www.decadentmini.com*
∗ Nathalie Tanghe 10br *www.etsy.com/shop/ polymerclaybox*

All step-by-step and other images are the copyright of Quarto Publishing plc. While every effort has been made to credit contributors, Quarto would like to apologize should there have been any omissions or errors and would be pleased to make the appropriate correction for future editions of the book.

PolymerClay.co.uk supplied a number of polymer clay tools and supplies used in the materials and techniques section of the book.
www.PolymerClay.co.uk

FIMO

With thanks to Staedtler (UK) Ltd. for supplying FIMO.
www.staedtler.co.uk

Some of the content in this book originally appeared in *Encyclopedia of Polymer Clay Techniques* by Sue Heaser, *Making Polymer Clay Beads* by Carol Blackburn and *The Polymer Clay Artist's Guide* by Marie Segal.

Author's acknowledgements
∗ The Make It Room: *www.themakeitroom.co.uk*
∗ Blooming Felt: *www.bloomingfelt.co.uk*
∗ Time for Tea Beads: *timeforteabeads.blogspot.co.uk*